ROBERTO
MANGABEIRA
UNGER

THE RELIGION OF THE FUTURE

Abridged and Edited,
with an Introduction by
MACABE KELIHER

Bridwell Press
Southern Methodist University
Dallas, Texas

Abridgment of *The Religion of the Future* by Roberto Mangabeira Unger

Published by Southern Methodist University, Bridwell Press (2023)
by arrangement with Harvard University Press.

Bridwell Press is the professional publishing arm of Bridwell Library
(SMU Libraries and Perkins School of Theology).

DOI: https://doi.org/10.3998/mpub.12824530

ISBN 978-1-957946-07-8 (hardback)
ISBN 978-1-957946-08-5 (paperback)
ISBN 978-1-957946-09-2 (ebook-pdf)
ISBN 978-1-957946-06-1 (ebook-epub)

Cover and interior design by Alicia Beebe
Cover art: *1988, Underwater Series, #9* © Robert Alexander

Printed in the United States of America

THE RELIGION OF THE FUTURE

CONTENTS

Preface

THE PRESENT BOOK is an abridgment of Roberto Mangabeira Unger's *The Religion of the Future.* It represents an edited version of the original that is complete in argument but reduced in size. Nearly three-quarters of the original text has been excised by my editor's pen in pursuit of a tighter and more succinct argument. I have cut much of the detail and many of the counterarguments but have preserved the core insights, analysis, and vision. Expositions were often shortened or removed, as were greater illustrations of points and long forays and discussion categorizing tenets of thought in philosophy and religion that served to draw out implications or initiate exchanges with thinkers of the past. These arguments are important, to be sure, and the reader is encouraged to take them up in their entirety in the original; they were here sacrificed in the pursuit of clarity and to give greater emphasis to the author's revolutionary argument about humanity and the religion of the future.

The structure of the book has been slightly altered in the process. Most notably, the number of chapters is reduced from seven to four. The three original chapters detailing the three different religious orientations of Unger's analysis have been shortened and combined into a single chapter that I have retitled "Three Orientations to Existence." It seemed to me that a unified overview of the religions in their differences, similarities, and problems fit best in a single chapter on the matter. A new appendage to the end of that chapter is a section originally found in the first chapter on common elements and problems of these orientations. The original fifth chapter, "Religious Revolution Now," was removed, and parts of the central argument for why a religious revolution is required today were moved to other chapters. The extended discussion of Christianity and the history of Christian thought was edited down and moved to an appendix, where it engages a discussion of the possibilities and shortcomings of Christianity as the religion of the future.

The original book had neither an introduction nor a conclusion, both of which I assembled from the author's prose. The introduction has been reconstructed from relevant passages in the text and relabeled as "Introduction: The Religion of the Future." Despite my rearranging of the author's structure and flow of writing, this introduction emerged organically from those places in the text where the author presented his argument or the themes of the book. I extracted those paragraphs and stitched them together into a coherent overview, all the while giving emphasis to the vision of the religion of the future. I have also included parts that prepare the argument rather than complement it, such as the general discussion of what religion is. While the introduction is a patchwork, the conclusion of the present volume is simply the slightly revised final three sections of the last chapter of the original book set on their own under the title "Conclusion" to better guide the reader. I have further taken the liberty to add subtitles throughout in order to highlight the key sections.

* * *

My endeavors in editing this book have been prompted by three motivations. Foremost is the vision and message of the book itself. Having read almost everything Unger has written in English, having absorbed hundreds of hours of his lectures and speeches, and having engaged him in endless conversations and discussions, this book, to my mind, represents the most comprehensive and forceful articulation of his ideas in both institutional and moral form, tying them to an understanding of human existence. In this text, Unger not only integrates his social theory and institutional program, which were developed in previous works, but also links it with a vision of humanity. In many ways, the book begins from the ground up with the fundamental question of being and systematically builds an understanding of self and society. It presents both spiritual and political programs, which lay the basis for individual and social change grounded in an inspiring vision of humanity. In short, it provides an answer to the big questions of who we are and how we ought to live our lives.

A second motivation is my use of this text in an undergraduate course on the history of early Chinese social and political thought. For the student initially encountering oracle bones and grappling with Warring States thinkers, *The Religion of the Future* offers a conceptual framework for understanding the various texts and practices under consideration by helping place ideas from a remote time and place alongside more familiar concerns, while at the same time pinning the texts to a root human condition. Thus, rather than regarding the questions and concerns of the *Mencius* as something only pertaining to itinerant Confucian politicians arguing in fourth-century-BCE royal courts, for example, *The Religion of the Future* helps to extract the universal and to situate it both conceptually and locally. Moreover, the book articulates a vision and a program for both individual existence and collective life, against which students can more easily measure those of the distant thinkers under consideration, whose discussions of monarchs, literati, rituals, and laws may not be as familiar. With these considerations, the abridgment aims to solicit the interest of the student and hold it firmly through the development of the argument on the religious orientations to existence and the articulation of a program of thought concerning self, society, and cosmos.

The third motivation is more personal and thus less formative to my edited text but perhaps just as important in the undertaking and its completion. I started engaging with Professor Unger and his ideas as a graduate student in 2010, around the time he began to articulate the foundations of the original book in a series of lectures that were further developed in his classes at Harvard College and Harvard Law School. Having witnessed the unfolding of the book over a number of years, I naturally became interested in its publication and dissemination and discussed it with him shortly after its release in 2014. Whether he broached the topic of an abridgment or I pressed him on the matter, I can no longer remember, for we were in agreement that a distillation of the core arguments would serve as a guide to initiate readers in the key ideas and hopefully provoke the interest of those unfamiliar with his thought. I undertook an initial edit of the original book at the time, but other professional and family obligations prevented me from completing the task. Now, in this second decade of the twenty-first century, as human society has endured a global pandemic that has forced us to confront the immediacy of our mortality and the limitations of our existing social institutions and practices, the need to take up the question of the religion of the future becomes ever more vital. That, and the time afforded by shutdowns, has finally driven the task to completion.

* * *

As a final word, I should say here that if I have been successful in my task as editor, this small volume will have made an adequate presentation of Unger's ideas insofar as they are set forth in *The Religion of the Future.* It would be most unfortunate, however, if this abridgment came to be regarded as an entirely satisfactory substitute for the original, for much of the scope of the argument and some of the insights have been simplified, along with the novel contributions to the history of thought and religion. As an easily accessible statement of Unger's complex ideas and his radical proposals regarding self and society, it is sufficient. But as an explication of the range of ideas and the potential implications they have on other systems of thought and action, it surely is not, as many lines of argument have been lost to the editor's perhaps overzealous hand. Only the big book, one feels, is worthy of the totality of the author's ideas, and, after having digested this abridgment, the reader will hopefully be inspired to turn to the original.

MK
Dallas, Texas
January 2021

Editor's Introduction

I

THE RELIGION OF THE FUTURE is, at its most basic level, a secular project for spiritual and political revolution. It presents a comprehensive vision of humanity and the broad outlines of a program for the refashioning of self and society in order to enable each man and woman to live a greater life. The project offers an outline for transforming social institutions as well as imperatives of moral practice with the aim of enhancing life, both individually and collectively. In doing so, it exhorts us to live in the present by embracing the life we have now rather than suppressing or trying to overcome our existential and spiritual limitations. The program to facilitate these aims involves both moral and political measures, the former concerned with an individual's conduct of life, or what is more commonly spoken of as moral philosophy, and the latter engaging the structure of society.

This introduction briefly outlines the four parts of the argument of this book – our existential flaws, the religious orientations and their limitations, the political program, and the moral program

– followed by an exploration of the intellectual background and ideas of the author and why he matters today. Those readers eager to engage the book itself are encouraged to skip this chapter and turn directly to Unger's introduction and the beginning of the text.

II

Who are we as human beings? How to face the existential misgivings that besiege our consciousness and the ambiguities that torment our souls? How should we live our lives? How ought we to relate to others?

The Religion of the Future begins with a reflection on the nature of who we are as human beings and the predicaments of our existence. Unger identifies three irreparable flaws in our existential constitution: death, groundlessness, and insatiability, as well as a fourth flaw, which is reparable, belittlement. These four defects of the human condition, he argues, inform the religious and intellectual programs of the past two millennia. Our mortality both terrifies and hinders us by forcing a reconciliation in the here and now with an impending and ineluctable end to consciousness and the meaning of our lives. Our inability to grasp the totality of the spiritual and material world sets us adrift on a groundless plane of contemplations and a steady fear of unknowns, not the least of which is the meaning of our own lives. Together, these feelings lead to an unquenchable thirst for more of something – anything – an insatiability in the immediacy of demands that can never be met, whether cravings of the mind or the flesh.

These three deficiencies, death, groundlessness, and insatiability, are accompanied, Unger argues, by a fourth defect of belittlement. Belittlement is the response to personal degradation under the weight of both our existential needs and the social roles within which we find ourselves. It is the outcome of a spiritual and material occlusion of transcendence from individual and social contexts, the drudgery and humiliation of existence or of poverty and social inferiority that frames the daily lives of the majority of men and women and forecloses any escape or alternative. Belittlement triggers the resignation of our situation, leading to bitterness in a confrontation with our existential mortality and relinquishing the time that we have in this world or by making peace with a socially inferior position and the humiliations it brings. It may also manifest in the form of avoidance, the abandonment of the self, for example, to the pleasures of flesh, food, or consumption.

Whereas mortality, groundlessness, and insatiability encase the human condition and cannot be alleviated, Unger holds, belittlement is avoidable and can be addressed by an adequate response. We can confront the three irreparable flaws in a way so that they do not obstruct the life that we have now, Unger argues, and furthermore we can restructure our social contexts to overcome belittlement so that we can reach for and fulfill aspirations and achieve a better life. These, then, are the grounds of religion: providing answers and responses to the irreparable flaws and overcoming the reparable one. The problem that Unger sees with existing religions, however, is that they have offered false solutions to the ineradicable features of human life while making compromises with belittlement.

In Unger's analysis, there are three main orientations to existence: overcoming the world, humanizing the world, and struggling with the world. These emerged in their religious forms during the Axial Age (500 BCE – 500 CE) and have continued to inform ideas about ourselves and the organization of our societies in various religious and philosophical systems up to the present day. Overcoming the world is best represented by Buddhism and early forms of Daoism, humanizing the world by Confucianism, and struggling with the world by the religions of salvation, particularly Christianity. Each orientation responds to the features of human existence in an attempt to come to terms with who we are as human beings and how we ought to live our lives. Each develops a program of being and interaction that is attached to a metaphysics offering an explanation of human beings within their social world and the cosmos.

Having set up the analysis, Unger then critiques the three orientations from two positions, religious and social. The problem of religion is its inadequate response to our existential flaws: despite the intentions of existing religions to address these flaws, they all develop positions that amount to a dismissal. Rather than facing our mortality, groundlessness, and insatiability, each orientation in its own way attempts to push them aside and develop different means to comfort us in the face of our fears. Death, for example, in each orientation, is not a provocation to us to make the most of the time we have in life but instead is posited as but a passing state or illusion, as in the case of Buddhism, or an opportunity to join a creator in heaven, as in Christianity. We are led to give up what we have in life now in order to cultivate ourselves for death and what lies beyond. Doing so robs us of life, Unger says, and leads to an insufficient response to the reparable flaw of belittlement by promoting acquiescence to the conditions and contexts of belittlement in the hope of future prospects. This is the social critique. Religion tells us, for example, not to fight to change the structural injustices of society but rather to simply help those in need and turn the other cheek in promise of a reward beyond this world.

These shortcomings implicate the more immediate one for moderns: how to change ourselves and our society. For over two millennia, Unger argues, our aspirations have been limited by the existing orientations in both spiritual and secular forms (he here implicates liberal democracy as a secular incarnation of the third orientation). Yet humanity continues to strive for something more than what these options have to offer, even as we remain wedded to them. Each generation works to surpass the previous one in a search and struggle for something more in both social organization and applicable understandings of our spiritual and material predicaments. Such strivings have generated modern science and critical philosophy, which have rendered the responses of the past incredible and virtually untenable. We have come to see ourselves as but a certain species of conscious animal living on one of possibly many habitable rocks in a far-off corner of space amid a vast universe that apparently has no interest in our well-being. This contemporary understanding of ourselves and the cosmos necessitates another response or set of responses to the human condition. Another orientation is necessary, Unger argues, one that does not simply make adjustments to the existing orientations but serves as a new religion of the future.

What is this religion of the future? More precisely, what are the incitements for a religion of the future? For Unger, it will need to embrace our irreparable flaws of mortality, groundlessness, and insatiability, rather than ameliorate or assuage them as do the existing orientations. In addition, it must provide means for grappling with and overcoming belittlement. In these terms, the religion of the future should allow us to share in the attributes that we often assign to the divine by enabling us to confront death and live a greater life here and now. It should empower us to transcend the limitations of our human existence by giving us the capacity to embrace and direct our irreparable flaws and to overcome our reparable one. In short, for Unger, the religion of the future must complete the religious revolutions of the past to "rescue humankind from its lack of imagination and love."[1] Its program needs to be both political and moral.

The political program of the religion of the future as outlined by Unger calls for the remaking of society so as to better realize the ascent of humanity. (Past religious revolutions, by contrast, accepted existing institutional structures and made compromises with organizational authority.) At the most basic level, this means promoting institutions for a free society whereby each individual is afforded the necessary education, welfare, and financial means not simply to sustain life but to facilitate the pursuit of a richer life. Unger cautions against the implementation of any particular set of institutions or societal structures, such as liberal democracy, because we are context-transcending beings by definition and must always retain the capacity to alter our institutions. Instead, he offers four principles to guide the religion of the future in institutional endeavors: apostasy, or the space to reject; plurality; freedom; and cooperation. Freedom is perhaps the most important, and Unger distinguishes between shallow and deep freedom. The former accepts existing social structures and attempts to find spaces of activity within – for example, freedom from government intrusion. The latter seeks to change those structures to realize individual and collective transcendence of circumstances – for example, developing mechanisms to facilitate challenge to constraints combined with the capacity to change the corresponding institutions.

The moral program of Unger's religion of the future moves from the reconstruction of society to a way of being that extols attitudes and practices, enabling us to share in the attributes of a greater life. This program has three sets of virtues by which we should live: connection, purification, and divinization, each of which is defined by a number of practices. The virtues of connection guide our relations with others; in doing so they are meant not as restraints upon selfishness but rather ways to engage others through respect, forbearance, fairness, and courage. The virtues of purification address the problem of belittlement in the face of our existential flaws through simplicity in material existence, enthusiasm in life, and attentiveness in the world. The virtues of divinization frame the self as embodied spirit and emphasize the means by which we can strive to transcend our contexts; they ask us to accept risk and vulnerability in embracing rather than shrinking from life and to open ourselves to others and to the new.

What the religion of the future must offer us is not comfort or consolation but more life – and not in the future but here and now. It must raise us up both individually and collectively, give us the political means to change our institutions and our circumstances, and provide the spiritual means to respond to our flaws with both love and imagination. As Unger puts it, such a religion of the future needs to make us both sweeter and greater.[2]

III

Roberto Mangabeira Unger is both a philosopher and a politician. He has published over a dozen books, each a probing intervention in such diverse intellectual fields as philosophy, social theory, law, economics, and cosmology. In each, he turns his inquiry not to the disciplines themselves or to related internal debates but rather to the foundations of knowledge about humans, societies, and nature. He has taught for almost half a century at Harvard Law School, where he became one of the youngest tenured faculty members in 1976 and has since instructed some of the world's leading academics and politicians. In his native Brazil, he was at the forefront of the democracy movement in the 1980s and more recently has served two terms as Minister of Strategic Affairs. For many years he has divided his time and energy between a life of the mind in Cambridge, Massachusetts, and a life of political action in Brazil.

In interviews and musings, Unger often remarks that he has been animated by the question of how to think and act in the world. His writings embrace a view of philosophy that regards it as the mind at war, struggling constantly with the ideas of previous intellectual giants. The corpus of his intellectual work sets out to develop a comprehensive view of who we are as human beings and to forge a path that will enable us individually and collectively to aspire to and realize a greater life. His task is undertaken by attempting to grasp the totality of human thought and categorize it in a system of views or visions pertaining to the questions at hand. Although he moves to catalog every thinker from Confucius to Nietzsche, his line of influence comes largely from the traditions of Christian philosophy, German idealism, British empiricism, and American pragmatism.[3]

As a politician, Unger has allowed action to shape his ideas of what is possible and has also moved to implement his intellectual conclusions. This has taken place over a forty-year career in Brazilian opposition politics as well as through interventions in progressive alternatives around the world. He helped establish the main opposition party in Brazil in the 1970s and wrote its founding manifesto. He also directed the presidential campaigns of Leonel Brizola and Ciro Gomes in the 1980s and '90s, ran for the Chamber of Deputies in the 1990s, and twice launched exploratory bids for the Brazilian presidency. His most established position was as Minister of Strategic Affairs, which he held in 2007–2009 and 2015 in the Lula and Dilma administrations.

IV

Roberto Mangabeira Unger was born in Rio de Janeiro on March 24, 1947, to a Brazilian mother and a German father. He grew up in New York City but spent summers in Brazil with his grandfather, Octávio Mangabeira, governor of the state of Bahia and then national senator. In his youth he would stay with the senior Mangabeira in the capital and every day walk with him the few blocks to the senate building, where he would sit in the gallery and listen to the speeches before returning home with his grandfather. "He would walk in the streets, people would kiss his hand, no one would accept money from him," Unger told an interviewer in 2008. "For me, it was a remarkable, potent image ... A person could be good and even saintly and nevertheless completely engaged in the world."[4] Of the time, he recalls:

> The experience of coming regularly from New York to this wild, exotic, ecstatic, big burst of life that was Brazil was irresistibly seductive to my imagination as a child...that was the experience that first aroused my passion for politics. You might say, it contaminated me at the very beginning with a romantic impulse... there are elements of truth in romanticism, and one of the elements of truth is this: that to set fire to the world you have to set fire to yourself. This is the truth of romanticism, and this is the truth that in some way I perceived very early through this vicarious experience of introduction to public life in Brazil.[5]

Unger claims to have been captivated by the deepest questions of human existence since as early as he can remember. He often cites his exposure to Plato at age seven: "My mother read to me at night, in little installments, Benjamin Jowett's translation of Plato's *Republic*. Ever since then, speculative thought has seemed to me to be the highest task of the mind."[6] Although speculative thought as the task of the mind of a seven-year-old sounds rather fanciful, what can be said is that at some point in his youth he began to read widely. He went systematically through the great thinkers of history, his program comprising three themes: classical social theory, philosophy, and literature. In classical social theory, Unger was especially influenced by Marx and cites *A Contribution to the Critique of Political Economy* as a key source of inspiration that opened his imagination to the denaturalization of the world. Weber's comparative history of religions and their relation to society also held great sway in his mind. In philosophy, Unger was most attracted to Aristotle and Hegel, because each offered a system to explain the world and everything in it. He also closely read Descartes, Spinoza, Kant, and Schopenhauer, aided by introductory works on these thinkers. In poetry, Unger was taken by Dante and Milton, and in literature, he found the European novel the most powerful exploration of humanity, especially from writers like Tolstoy, Dostoevsky, Flaubert, Proust, and Eliot.

There was, however, something else driving Unger: a struggle with his Christian faith. He had grown up cultivating religious learning, developing a devotion to theology, attending mass, and exploring the teachings of the Catholic Church. But when he was eleven, his father died of a heart attack, precipitating a crisis in the preadolescent Unger and shaking the foundations of his belief in God and the teachings of the church. It was a crisis intensified by an early adolescent rebellion against the world in an attempt to find his place in it. Unger turned away from doctrine to philosophy and literature to answer questions about the flaws of human existence, gradually replacing his Christian metaphysics with a radical politics of self and society.

The narrative of Unger's education overlaps his loss of faith. Once the idea of God and the doctrines of religion are rejected, something has to take their place. It may be unreflective modern science, crude atheism, or even a collection of ideas and beliefs surrounding, for example, magic that is taken up to inform an understanding of the universe. The individual, burdened by more than mere curiosity about the self and the world, is confused, terrified of death, overwhelmed by the vastness of the universe and the finite time given to inquire of it, and filled with an insatiable desire to know, to make sense of life, and to demand more from himself and others. The religions of the world, as the pages below argue, have notably given answers to the questions posed by the human condition, offering a vision and a set of practices by which people might orientate their lives. It was these answers that the young Unger latched onto and that had provided meaning, but it was also these that he had to discard in the face of the contradictions found in his immediate experience. Along with the casting off of the Christian faith went the entire metaphysical system of understanding and knowledge that had been the basis of Unger's religion.

Although he initially turned to philosophy to bring light to the world and his position in it, Unger rejected traditional views of the discipline. He came to see philosophy as practiced throughout much of its history as a kind of would-be super-science in the service of self-help. It offered speculative answers to the human condition and the fundamental flaws of our existence – what Unger terms our mortality, groundlessness, and insatiability – and presented a foundational view that enables us to respond to the anxieties and torments of our existence. In our contemporary age, however, we have lost confidence in any ideal of who we are, rejecting all attempts at establishing foundational knowledge of our condition. This has led philosophy to degenerate into, as Unger calls it, a "thought police," a scholastic clarification of arguments that tells us how we can and cannot speak. But for Unger, "philosophy as we should conceive it today is the mind at war, rebelling against all the constraints imposed on it by the established disciplines and the predominant methods and insisting on its prerogative to deal with the things that matter most."

V

While the experience of death led him to the philosophers of the past, the memory of his politically active grandfather took him into law. In his late adolescence, Unger envisioned becoming a thinker and writer with a position at a university while also maintaining a public life as a jurist. With this in mind, Unger, right out of high school, went into a five-year law program at the Federal University of Brazil and then into the LL.M. program at Harvard Law School, where he wrote a thesis that would serve as the basis of a core chapter in his first book, *Knowledge and Politics.*

Upon the completion of his program at Harvard, Unger anticipated returning to Brazil. But that year, 1970, saw the Brazilian military dictatorship adopt extreme counterinsurgency tactics to combat the growing militarization of opposition groups. Many of Unger's extended family, including his grandfather's brother, who was the minister of justice and a leftist agitator against the dictatorship, were stripped of political rights. Unger's sister, who was part of the revolutionary underground, was arrested in a shootout and seriously injured in the process, slipping into a coma. Unger's family cautioned him against returning, and because the dictatorship had stripped him of his passport, he could not return even if he wanted to.

Given the extremity of the situation, Harvard offered Unger a fellowship that would enable him to stay on. The law faculty created a year-long fellowship position that allowed him to conduct research and then, in the midst of that fellowship year, the law school offered him a job to begin the following year with the appointment of assistant professor. It was in this way, at age twenty-three years , that Unger began teaching jurisprudence to first-year Harvard Law School students, most of whom were his own age. In his second year, he took on teaching "Contracts," the year-long slog through the basics of doctrinal law, during which he developed the core ideas that informed the first half of his book *The Critical Legal Studies Movement.*

Over the next four years, Unger worked on his first two books, *Knowledge and Politics* and *Law in Modern Society.* They appeared in quick succession in 1975 and 1976, respectively, and both met with much critical acclaim in law journal reviews. Their publication led to him receiving the prestigious Guggenheim Fellowship in 1976 and then tenure at Harvard. At twenty-nine years old, he became one of the youngest faculty members to obtain tenure, an honor that he would not vaunt but that would give him the space to pursue his intellectual projects.[7]

One of the most consequential intellectual projects of the day was the Critical Legal Studies movement, or CLS. The movement was a reaction in American law schools to the dominant legal ideology and came to overturn the methodological orthodoxy of legal thought. Whereas American legal realism had previously reigned as the methodological consensus in law schools, the Crits, as the proponents of the movement came to be called, championed a pluralism that untethered the legal discipline from any single methodology or practice.[8] In a series of articles Unger and other Crits attacked the legal establishment for taking an instrumental view of law as a mechanism to objectively resolve conflict and facilitate interactions.[9] They argued instead that law was not neutral and that judges did not simply apply the law; rather bias was inherent in adjudication.[10] Spurred on, the movement grew in the 1970s and '80s and quickly moved out of the Harvard Law quad to schools across the country.

Unger came to criticize the direction of the movement. He rejected the two forms that CLS had taken, a neo-Marxist functionalism, which explained law as but a function of power to uphold the structures of capitalism, and a radical indeterminism, which understood law to mean anything that anybody wanted it to mean – the equivalent of finding meaning on the back of a cereal box. Neither of these directions had a constructivist agenda, he argued. "Both have yet to take a clear position on the method, the content, and even the possibility of prescriptive and programmatic thought," Unger wrote in the bibliographic note to his book, *The Critical Legal Studies Movement,* adding that this was the case "because some of the assumptions inherited from the radical tradition make it hard to turn constructive proposals into more than statements of commitment or anticipations of history."[11] He then moved to stake out a view of law that viewed it not as an isolated aspect of structure that was detached from other areas of life – something that exists as merely another part of society – but rather as residing within the very structures of society. Law for Unger is the site that determines the form of the institutions that represent social interests and ideals; it can serve as the forum for institutional experimentation in pursuit of alternatives.

VI

Until the late 1970s, Unger's life had been devoted to ideas. Apart from accompanying his grandfather to the senate and observing his interactions with constituents, Unger had devoted himself to study and the development of thought. Then in 1977, Unger began to engage with the Brazilian left. He worked to help end the military dictatorship in 1985 and then to implement institutional alternatives. In the course of doing so, he hoped not just to change Brazilian society and offer a better, freer life for ordinary Brazilians but also to develop the theories and practices that could be applied throughout Latin America and the world. Here began for him the intersection of theory and practice. Over the next ten years, political involvement would come to shape his social theory and contribute to the full development of a revolutionary program that moved beyond liberalism and Marxism.

The measured practice of philosophy and politics has long overlapped in the history of thought, to be sure, and they have done so in a sort of dialectic between theory and practice, especially during times of crisis. Plato and Aristotle developed their political philosophy in the face of a declining Athenian state, Saint Augustine wrote in the midst of the demise and fall of the Roman Empire, as did Machiavelli during the political decay of Italy. Hobbes and Locke grappled with the aftermath and meaning of the English Revolution, while French thinkers like Montesquieu and Rousseau wrote in the time of the end of monarchy and in view of revolution. German idealists like Kant, Fitche, and Hegel attempted to come to terms with new political formations, and the liberals and socialists of the nineteenth century looked at the emergence of the social phenomenon of the masses and the viciousness of absolutism. In each of these cases, thought was inspired by political developments, while also seeking to intervene in shaping the course of politics.[12]

The most fervent political theorizing often emerges in times of political decline.[13] In all of the examples cited above, the thinker in question faced social and political changes such that politics as practiced could no longer produce results of control and command. Political theorists thus saw the need to develop and explain the possibility of an alternative and to theorize beyond the practical limitations of current politics. This was precisely the situation encountered by Unger in the 1980s: the breakdown of military rule and the emergence of compromises that could not contain the struggles and reality of Brazilian society. These developments could neither be contained by existing politics nor explained by existing political theory. Faced with a situation of "the country in a daze," as he called it, Unger rejected existing social thought and set about developing anew a revolutionary social theory.[14] He constructed institutional alternatives and worked to create the opportunity to implement them in order to realize a freer society and a more radical democracy.

When the military regime in Brazil dissolved the two-party system and multi-party elections in 1980, Unger worked to unite progressives, liberals, and the noncommunist independent left. The party that emerged was the Party of the Brazilian Democratic Movement (PMDB). As cofounder, Unger wrote its first manifesto, which translated his social and political ideas into the language of party politics, emphasizing the need to open institutions to facilitate greater change and development. "Through democratization and mobilization," he wrote, "all society would become not the fulfillment of some ultimate destiny but a field experiment." The key tenets of the manifesto resist the hardening of a particular form of society and call for flexibility and plasticity to allow individuals and groups to organize themselves in new and creative ways. In the political realm, he pointed to the importance, and also the insufficiency, of constitutional democracy, emphasizing that the achievement of a new constitution was not the end goal but rather a first step in an ascent. In the economy, the manifesto called for a transformation of the means of production, moving from large corporations to small and medium enterprises. In accordance, there was a need to avoid polarization between organized workers and the petty bourgeoisie and between rural and urban workers. In each of these areas, and strung throughout the entire document, was the prevalence of the idea that institutions and practices are not a blueprint but rather a provisional stage in the fight for a greater life and a freer society.[15]

In 1981, Unger left the party. "It had lost its character," he said. What Unger wanted was a political agent who could serve as the vehicle for a national alternative, a statesman who would be receptive to the advice of a philosopher. That year he met Leonel Brizola, the governor of Rio de Janeiro and a figure of the left, and joined his Democratic Labor Party (PDT). Unger saw Brizola and his party as the authentic opposition to the military regime with a political path forward, both in terms of a progressive opposition and as a party to promote his ideas and programmatic agenda. In 1985, the PMDB won the presidency but did so on an institutionally conservative platform, leading Unger to write a series of articles attacking the PMDB and arguing for economic, social, and constitutional alternatives. The critiques, analysis, and alternatives put forward at that time served as the basis of his social theory, which he developed in full in the pages of *Politics*.[16]

In Unger's analysis, three groups, roughly divided along the spectrum of right, center, and left, fought over the direction of the country. Foremost, a group of conservatives sought to maintain the status quo in terms of political liberalization and state-control over the economy. This entailed support for large agriculture companies, a manufacturing industry that produced for the wealthy, and a regime funded by export revenue and foreign capital. Their response to poverty and economic deprivation was to stimulate growth by encouraging investment through lower taxation. The second group was to the center-left of the conservatives and included a coalition advocating redistribution. This included the PMDB, which developed an agenda of fiscal, income, and welfare policies to redistribute wealth through the existing structures by means of the various social institutions. The third group advocated institutional change and included the PDT and the left PMDB. However, the problem with this last group, Unger argued, was that it put the conquest of state power before the transformation of society.

These three groups based their politics on the philosophies of state and society available to them, namely, liberalism or socialism. The conservatives took up an agenda of greater liberalization of the economy in order to spur economic growth and pursue unfettered investment and the building of wealth. The left sought institutional change through the seizure of state power and the use of the government to push a particular social agenda. While these models provided the immediate inspiration for the shaping of society and a direction that it could take, they did not match the social reality and the nature of social and economic relationships in Brazil. The visions and the institutional forms being fought over were limited by the ideas at hand, limitations that retarded the people's aspirations. As Unger put it, "Ideas spoiled the quest for power."[17]

Beyond the parties, the traditional politics of left and right did not fit the emergent situation. In Brazil, and throughout the world, it was becoming clear that the middle class did not necessarily hold interests and ideals different from the working class; the working classes were not necessarily divided along lines of race, gender, or urban/rural, and organized labor was not necessarily pitted against unorganized workers and the unemployed. These distinctions undermined revolution in the Western world and generated resistance to structural transformation as different interests clashed and fought for the preservation of their positions. The lack of such distinctions in Brazil meant that a new kind of politics could emerge, one that was not premised on the primacy of one form of life or labor and that held out the possibility of the birth of a plurality of groups and the realization of new interests pointing to new forms of organization in work and life. All this required a new social theory.

VII

Unger's thought begins at the very beginning, with conceptions of being and of who we are as humans. For Unger, we are beings of infinite depth trapped in a finite context. Within each of us is more than the limited conception of a contained individual defined or captured by our immediate contexts. Historically, this has been termed the soul or the embodied spirit and carries with it the idea that each of us possesses unique individuality of boundless becoming that no single form of life can express and which neither assigned social role nor social station can define. At the same time, we live in a world that places restrictions on our actions, that attempts to define and limit who we are. Cast in a role, of a son or daughter, for example, or of a student or teacher, we are led to believe that we must perform it: we are mistaken in the notion that this is who we are and that we must embody it. With respect to each role, expectations are attached, behaviors are associated, actions are prescribed. A way of life is defined and people are told that this is the limit of their being. Unger, rejecting this limitation, holds that we are infinite: "There is always more in us than there are in them [the roles or structures]." And: "We must deny them the last word and keep the last word for ourselves."[18]

This vision of self has implications for social theory. If our beings have no natural form – that is, no essential human nature – and cannot be reconciled with any given context, then there is no social structure that can do us justice. Neither liberalism, socialism, communism, social democracy, nor any other organization of society can offer a suitable home for our restless beings. We have no natural context. Any set of social arrangements and their institutions are poor artifacts that will necessarily limit the realization of our humanity and capabilities. In this way, the blueprints offered by various political ideologies and constitutions of the past two hundred years are built upon a static notion of human nature; they attempt to force our individual and social beings into an idealized form of human nature and of how the social world should work. They do not capture who we are, and, worse, they limit us. Unger terms this vein of thought "false necessity."

With this move, Unger pushes to the hilt the insight that society is made and imagined. He strips away the blueprint and in its place offers a vision of who we are and an idea of impermanent institutions that are open to revision. The institutions that mediate our interactions – the state, the market, the social order – should maximize the individual and the collective powers of humanity. They should serve us rather than we them. In this way, in Unger's thought, any political, social, or economic institution needs a mechanism that gives us the ability to reform and revise it so that "the dead do not rule over the living." This is what Unger calls a structure of no structure. It is the realization a context that can be constantly remade – that is, the idea that institutions can lend themselves to frequent experimentation so that constraints are abrogated as soon as they arise and we are always empowered over our context.

What this might look like and how to achieve it are the subject of the third part of Unger's system of ideas, programmatic proposals and disciplinary interventions. He holds that the institutional form of democracy must be loosened so that political life can be immediately accessible to every individual and society wide structural change can be proposed and enacted. This might begin with ending the checks and balances of the executive and legislative branches so that the party in power can push through a reform agenda. In the realm of the economy, Unger advocates a democratization of the market whereby "more people have more access to more markets." This begins with the expansion of credit and the broadscale sharing of technology and managerial knowledge. Both of these proposals must be accompanied by reforms in education so that students are instructed in analytical capabilities to disrupt and innovate and are treated as "tongue-tied prophets" rather than blank slates on which to inscribe the rules of social and political order. The role of legal thought in all of this, Unger holds, is that of helping devise the institutional form of these programs, such as how, for example, alternative market regimes would look.

Beyond structure, our lives and social worlds are premised on individual consciousness and human relations that prompt the question of how to live in society. For Unger, we view others through a lens of contradiction. On one hand, we need other people – we need to relate to them, find commonality with them, and receive confirmation of ourselves through them. Through our relationships with others, we hope to grow more aware of ourselves and freer of our constraints. On the other hand, we are radically ambivalent toward others, fearing that our associations with them will subject us to belittlement or even enslavement. Given this tension, how then, should we relate to others? Unger's response – his ethics, if you will – is to advocate vulnerability, love, and cooperation. Vulnerability entails leaving ourselves open to challenge and change and refusing to submit ourselves to the roles in which we are cast.

Love in our immediate relations with others, he holds, should be among equals and on equal terms. The cooperation Unger envisions is that in our personal dealings and our work relations by which we come together as free and equal individuals, both instrumentally for the task at hand and communally in a show of solidarity.[19]

At the core of this vision of self, others, society, and politics is the denial of any natural or necessary form. Our natures are infinite and our societies always open to new types of arrangements and innovations. There is no predetermined ideal form, no script, and no evolution toward the best possible system. Nor is there a moral imperative to mediate our dealings with each other. If we are free and the new is possible, we must ask how we can reconcile this vision of humanity with nature and natural laws. Rejecting the dualism of Descartes and Kant, which posited humanity as separate from nature, Unger holds that we are a part of nature and that nature and natural laws are as subject to change as is our social world. In Unger's thought, the laws of nature are mutable, as are those of society. For him, the only constant is time, which subjects the whole universe to a history, a history that recognizes causation and is open to the new.

This is the core of Unger's thought.

VII

Imagine, for a moment, that you have been born in a poor village in a developing country. You are doomed to a life of poverty. You have minimal educational opportunities and no access to jobs, money, or credit. If you are lucky enough to scrape together funds to travel to a major industrial city to get your name on a list for factory hires, and if you are then chosen from among the thousands of other migrant workers in the same situation, you may be able to earn a hundred dollars a month working ten to twelve hour days, six days a week. The work will be repetitive manual labor, and if you do not lose an appendage or contract some malady from the toxic, unregulated, unsafe working conditions, your specific skill will likely become obsolete in ten years. You will then become unemployable and part of a lost generation.

This is the reality for the majority of individuals around the world today. In some places, it is worse. This reality stands in stark contradiction to the paragon models that we have about ourselves and the world we want to live in. It tragically clashes with the aspirations we hold and expect of our social, political, and economic institutions. We hold fast to classical liberal ideals about individuals and their freedoms. We want our world to be one in which any hard-working and determined individual can be successful and raise her station in life. We see such beliefs infused throughout popular culture around the world, from Hollywood movies to Korean soap operas to Bollywood music videos. The story of the individual overcoming unsurmountable odds or of the lovers defying social constraints stimulates our fantasies and aspirations. We want to believe that we are empowered, that we are beings of infinite depth and cannot be contained by the impositions of the actually existing world. We want to believe that no context can hold us back and that opportunity is ours for the taking.

Herein lies Unger's project. His animating inquiries all serve an overarching aim of developing a view of ourselves that is empowering and arriving at a vision about how to remake our world and master our social contexts. Unger's project rethinks who we are as human beings – our desires and our capabilities – and presents a prophecy of humanity as the embodied spirit. To have a vision of humanity and its empowerment necessitates a vision about society and how our social world works, how it fits together, and how it changes. The institutions and their arrangements must be rethought and remade if we are to realize our individual and collective empowerment and actualize our full potential.

The problem is that the institutions that now order our world do not do this. Democracy, as it is now practiced in its institutional form of periodic elections and a disengaged electorate does not do justice to our ideals. The spiritually impoverished market economy and its dogmatic adherence to a certain conception of free trade put us at the mercy of finance and enslave us in wage labor. The individualism that structures our society does not enable us to be who we really are and to find solidarity with each other, but instead passes off this task to compensatory redistribution of wealth through tax and transfer. Alternative ideas and institutional forms are needed that better conform to our ideals, such innovations as democratic institutions that raise the temperature of politics, enable radical reform, and encourage ongoing debate about who we are and what we want to become. Indeed, we need an economy that enables experimentation with different kinds of market and financial regimes. We need social institutions that account for who we are collectively as well as individually and which maximize our tendencies and desires for solidarity. We need a new orientation to ourselves and our social worlds that takes account of our aspirations and lifts us up.

What we get from such maximalist projects are social arrangements and individual practices that enable us to take control of our lives and communities. What we get is the ascent of humanity – not just for some but for all. What we get is more life now.

INTRODUCTION

The Religion of the Future

THE ENHANCEMENT of life is our chief interest. In the pursuit of this interest we must seek to die only once.

What this purpose implies for the way in which we live and how we deal with ourselves and one another, and for the relation of this way of living to the reorganization of society, is among the major topics of this book. The commitment to die only once inspires a certain way of escaping belittlement. It also guides a response to each of the incidents in the course of life that threaten to make us accept belittlement as the corollary of finitude: our early expulsion from the center of the world, our confinement to a particular trajectory and station, and our threatened encasement and slow dying within a shell of character and compromise. The enhancement of life is central to what I here call the religion of the future.

The approach to existence that results from this argument does not deny the relation of morals to politics. The vision informing it can be enacted only to the extent that we move toward the ideal of deep freedom and embrace the institutional changes that the achievement of this ideal requires. The political program of deep freedom has consequences for the reconstruction of society in the present, not just in a remote future. Nevertheless, it is a collective task that advances or fails in historical time, not in the biographical time in which we as individuals must live and die. The less far we go in the transformation of society the greater is the weight that must be borne by self-transformation.

THE FLAWS OF HUMAN EXISTENCE

We must face the terrifying truth about our situation. Our confrontation with three great terrors of human life shakes and arouses us. These three terrors are the irreparable flaws of human existence: death, groundlessness, and insatiability. There is also a fourth flaw, belittlement, which is not an irreparable flaw but in fact curable.

The vital distinction to be drawn between the insuperable limitations of mortality, groundlessness, and insatiability and the corrigible defect of our susceptibility to belittlement helps make clear my aims in this book. My argument has two central themes, which are but aspects of the same conception. The first theme is the relation between our acceptance of death, groundlessness, and insatiability and our rejection of belittlement as a moral and a political endeavor. The second theme is the nature and direction of a religion of the future. The religion of the future is to be created through a series of innovations different in method as well as in content from those that generated the world religions of today. It is also a religion about the future. It concerns the bearing of the future on the present. It calls us to live for the future as a way of living in the present – as beings unconfined by the circumstances of our existence.

The statement and enactment of such a program offer our best hope of overcoming belittlement without deceiving ourselves about death, groundlessness, and insatiability. The two themes of the book are two sides of the same reality. It is crucial to any religion that it mark in the right place the division between the inalterable circumstances of existence and the alterable arrangements of society. To represent flawed and revisable ways of organizing social life as inescapable is the characteristic form of superstition about society and history: the illusion of false necessity. The consequence of such illusion is to entrench a particular ordering of society against challenge and transformation – it is to leave our ideals and interests hostage to the institutions and practices that represent them at a particular moment and thereby inhibit our efforts to reconsider their meaning. (A contemporary example of such institutional fetishism is the unwarranted identification of the abstract ideas of a market economy or of representative democracy with a particular, path-dependent way of organizing markets and democracies.)

Our mortality, unrelieved by any prospect of discerning the ground of existence, will make life, in every moment, all the more precious. Our groundlessness, lived under the shadow of our mortality, will discredit and undermine any attempt to ground a regime of society or of thought in a story about the nature of things. Our insatiability will teach us that the finite ends for which we grasp are never enough to content us, but only so many stopping points along the way. To deny these inescapable features of existence is to commit no less grievous an insult against ourselves. In failing to confront them we cease to awaken to a greater life from the sleepwalking of compromise, conformity, and the petrified self. We seize upon devices and stratagems that divide and enslave us under the pretext of empowering us.

THREE ORIENTATIONS TO EXISTENCE

In the early chapters of this book I explore three major spiritual orientations exemplified by the world religions. I call these orientations overcoming the world, humanizing the world, and struggling with the world. My purpose in this categorization is to prepare the ground for the defense of a way of thinking that goes beyond what these orientations have in common.

My argument can be read as an essay in the philosophy of religion, except that it is itself religious, and not simply an inquiry undertaken from the safe distance of uncommitted speculative thought. It might also be viewed as a theological text, except that it is a kind of anti-theology.

It is in no way a comparative and historical study of religion. I take some of the major world religions as prime instances of each of the three spiritual orientations that I consider: early Buddhism, which I situate under the term overcoming the world; early Confucianism as humanizing the world; and the Semitic monotheisms, especially Christianity, as struggling with the world. My interest in this preliminary part of the argument is not in the doctrinal content or the historical development of these religions but rather in the internal architecture of each of these spiritual orientations: its presuppositions, its core vision, and its approach to existence. Each of them, although primarily associated with certain religious traditions, remains a living spiritual option for any man or woman, anywhere and anytime.

These religions arose from a series of spiritual innovations or revolutions that occurred across more than a thousand years, from the beginnings of prophetic Judaism in the eighth century BC to the rise of Islam in the seventh century AD. They diverged radically from one another. Nevertheless, they shared important common ground: the commonalities are all the more striking in light of the depth of the divergence. I will emphasize these shared elements for a polemical and programmatic reason as well as for their intrinsic importance. The direction for which I argue breaks with this common ground in some ways while clinging to it in others. In the presentation of these views, I repeatedly refer to the religious revolutions of the past and contrast them in practice and doctrine with a religious revolution of the future.

I argue that the religion of the future must break with these orientations and the religious revolutions of the past. Above all, it must rebel against the ground that they share in common. If it finds more inspiration in one of them than in the others, it must nevertheless learn from the criticism of what it repudiates.

In the following pages, I explore the internal architecture of these major spiritual options. I do so with the intention of going beyond them, not with the aim of making claims about the distinctive doctrines and singular histories of the particular religions that have expressed them. Here the historical allusions remain ancillary to a philosophical and theological argument. The argument is chiefly concerned with the choice of a direction. I call this direction the religion of the future.

REASONS FOR RELIGIOUS REVOLUTION

In what sense are the shifts that I defend religious at all? In what sense do they amount to a revolution? There was once a time when we did not view the world in light of the ideas of the orientations of the religious revolutions. There is every reason to suppose that there will be a time in which their light, if not extinguished, will not be the sole or even the predominant influence on our most comprehensive beliefs about the human situation.

The gates of prophecy are never closed. It is contrary to all sense, and above all to the historical sense that represents one of the greatest achievements of the last few centuries, to suppose that religious revolution will happen only once in human history. Men and women have shown themselves capable of it in the past. Not even our faithlessness has destroyed this capability, or at least our prospect of once again acquiring it.

The overriding force that drives the development of religion is the need to commit our lives in one direction or another, on the basis of a view of the world and of our place in it and in response to the manifest facts of our mortality, groundlessness, and insatiability. The weight of such a commitment is only increased by the insufficiency of the grounds that we can ever hope to have for making it. The concerns that lead us to take such a stand are lasting and even irresistible; but even our most comprehensive answers to existence remain perpetually open to contest and revolution.

For over two millenniums, the spiritual experience of humanity has largely moved within the limits set by the three orientations: overcoming of the world, the humanization of the world, and the struggle with the world. This range of spiritual alternatives no longer suffices to contain the spiritual ambitions of humanity. It fails to do so for the reasons that I explore in the chapters below. These reasons supply the incitement for a future religious revolution and suggest its direction.

THE RELIGION OF THE FUTURE

The religion of the future must begin in the unwavering recognition of our existential flaws: our mortality, our groundlessness, and our insatiability. Without such recognition it cannot advance in its commitments. In particular, it cannot advance in the search for a greater existence. This then is the simple criterion of advance in the history of religion: that our future religion will cease to take as its maxim the attempt to make the irremediable defects in our existence seem less real and less frightening than they in fact are. An uncompromising acknowledgment of these flaws must be one of the starting points. The first requirement of our ascent to a greater life is to accept the truth about our circumstance and to reject consolation. To mark the path of a religious revolution defended by this standard is one of the goals of this book.

The reason for which the acknowledgment and acceptance of the defects in the human condition are central to any future religion is that such awareness can awaken us to life now. The fear of death, the shadow of nihilism, and the force of insatiable desire arouse us from the state of diminished consciousness in which our lives may otherwise be consumed. Spinoza wrote that a wise man's thoughts are directed to life rather than to death. However, by averting our attention from the ephemeral and dreamlike character of our existence, we lose the most powerful instrument with which we can hope to resist surrender to routine, repetition, and petty compromise. Death-bound, distracting ourselves with the diversions that enable us to forget or even to deny our mortality, and forgetful of the mysterious character of our existence, we readily allow ourselves to be diminished. Life then seeps away, little by little.

By refusing to turn away from the defects in our existence, we arouse ourselves from our diminishment of existence. Our belittlement, which already weighed on us, now becomes intolerable. Every moment that goes by while we await our doom seems full and precious. The sight of death helps bring us fully to life.

The German soldiers who carried Heidegger's *Being and Time* around with them in the First World War did not need the ideas of that philosopher to lift themselves from the sleepwalking of everyday experience. They had war to remind them that at every moment they were death-bound. The words on the page mattered for a few because they seemed to give voice to an experience of terror that many experienced without having read them.

How is the religion of the future to shape our experience so that we no longer require the devotions of war – or of any other limiting and terrifying experience – to come to life? Society and culture must be so organized that they diminish the distance between the ordinary moves that we make within an institutional or ideological framework that we take for granted and the exceptional moves by which we challenge and change pieces of that framework. Our normal science, for example, must acquire some of the features of revolutionary science. Our education must be designed to school the mind in ideas and visions remote from those that prevail in the established culture and to free it from passivity and subservience by exposing it, at every turn, to contrasting points of view. Our democracies must be arranged in ways that increase the temperature of politics (that is, the level of organized popular engagement in political life) and hasten its pace (that is, the ability to break deadlock and bring about structural reform), diminishing the dependence of change upon crisis. Our market economies must favor an organization of work by which tasks are redefined in the course of being executed and an organization of the market economy in which we are free to innovate in the arrangements of production and exchange as well as in combinations of people, technologies, and capital.

WHAT RELIGION IS, OR HAS BEEN

In addressing the major spiritual orientations to have emerged over the last two millenniums and in presenting a view of what can and should succeed them, I use the contested concept of religion. To count as religion, a set of enacted beliefs or belief-informed practices must have three characteristics.

A first characteristic of religion is to respond to the incurable flaws in our existence: our movement toward death, our inability to place our existence in a definitive context of understanding and meaning, and the emptiness and insatiability of our desires. To these flaws we are wrongly tempted to add (wrongly because we can redress it) the disproportion between the force of our circumstances and the reach of our nature, e.g., belittlement. Whether the response offered by religion to these defects is one that robs them of their sting or on the contrary acknowledges them unflinchingly remains an issue at stake in the unfinished history of religion.

A second characteristic of religion is that it relates an orientation to life to a vision of our place in the world. The link between orientation and vision provides a kind of answer to the incorrigible defects in our circumstance. The answer recognizes the defects as more or less real and more or less susceptible to redress or response. It interprets their implications for the conduct of life. The vision acquires its power to guide because it addresses what is most disturbing in our existence: that we must die although we feel that we should not; that we seem unable, by the light of the understanding, to place our lives in a reliable context of meaning; that we always remain at the mercy of desires that are both empty and unlimited and that pursue us until our final end; and that little or nothing that we can do with our lives seems adequate to our context-transcending powers. The position that we take with respect to these problems acquires prescriptive authority. It enjoys such force both because of their intrinsic importance and because the way in which we deal with them has consequences for every other aspect of our experience.

A third characteristic of religion is that it requires us to commit our lives in a certain direction, and it requires us to do so without having what could ever be an adequate basis. If the position to take were only cognitive, we might be able to take no position at all. However, it is not merely cognitive; it goes to our need to form an attitude, implicit and unelaborated if not explicit and fully formed, to the most disturbing and perplexing aspects of our condition. We will have an attitude, whether we want to or not and whether we are fully conscious of the ideas informing it or not. In arriving at such an attitude, however, we are condemned to cognitive overreach: we must stake the course of our lives on suppositions whose grounds fail to do justice to the gravity of their implications and to the scope of their claims. This inescapable cognitive overreach, imposed on us by our circumstance, is what the vocabulary of the Semitic monotheisms calls faith.

A VISION FOR RELIGIOUS REVOLUTION

This book develops a vision responsive to the incitements of the religious revolution that I have discussed in this introduction. This vision does not rely on the family of beliefs long viewed in the West as the hallmark of religion, namely, faith in a transcendent God who created humans and the world and continues to intervene in history. From the perspective of those who define religion as such, the orientation to life for which I here argue is no religion at all. It nevertheless satisfies all the criteria that I have laid out in this section: it grounds an approach to existence in a vision of the world; it responds to the irreparable flaws in the human condition; and it requires faith.

Life, not harmony, is the watchword for a reorientation of our experience – we can make selves only by defying and changing structures of society and of thought. We become more human only by becoming more godlike. More than a humanization of society, the religion of the future seeks a divinization of humanity.

CHAPTER 1

Beyond Wishful Thinking: Life Without Illusion

DEATH

EVERYTHING IN OUR EXISTENCE points beyond itself. We must nevertheless die. We cannot grasp the ground of being. Our desires are insatiable. Our lives fail adequately to express our natures. Our circumstances regularly subject us to belittlement.

Religion has been both an attempt to interpret the meaning of these irreparable flaws in the human condition and a way of dealing with them. It has told us that everything is ultimately all right. Yet everything is not all right.

A turn in the religious consciousness of humanity would begin in an approach to these defects that would abandon the impulse to deny them. Religion would cease to console us for these frightening facts and instead confirm life, the greatest good. For with life comes surfeit, spontaneity, and surprise: the capacity to see more, make more, and do more than all the social and conceptual regimes in which we move can countenance. In the face of all constraint, the experience of life is an experience of a fecundity and a fullness without foreordained limits.

Everyone dies anyway. The response of nature to our experience of fecundity is to decree our death. The finality of this annihilation – in contrast to the vibrant presence that preceded it – is the first and fundamental reason why death is terrible. The good that is the highest is the good that will be most definitively destroyed. It precedes all others and makes all others possible.

Our fall toward death is surrounded on every side by tokens of the wasting of life. At any given moment on our planet, countless living creatures tear one another apart the better to live a while longer. We are unable to distinguish our situation from theirs as much as we would like. Science teaches that death forms part of the continuance of life. However, what is necessary for the species is fatal to the individual.

The hour of death comes sometimes with agitation and suffering and sometimes with resignation or even in sleep. Some people report, from near death experiences, that they see a great light. However, there is no great light, other than in the minds of some of the dying. According to certain conjectures, they perceive such a light because the brain is starved of oxygen or because there is stimulation, as life wanes, of the temporal lobe, as if the body, on the very verge, were playing a final trick on us.

Regardless of whether death is resisted or accepted, its aftermath follows a regular course. The body is now a corpse. It becomes first rigid, then bloated. It soon rots, stinks, and begins to be devoured by vermin and bacteria unless it is promptly burned. From having been revered, it turns into an object of revulsion. Here life ends in a strange sacrifice. Each of us is brought to the altar. This time no angel stays Abraham's hand. What is the point of the sacrifice and what faith does it serve? It is an incident in a cult, the secrets and purpose of which remain forever closed to us.

It is all the more terrifying to know that those whom we love will die, sometimes under our eyes. In their death we see what we can only imagine for ourselves: the annihilation, to which we are all doomed, confirmed as love proves powerless to sustain the life that love may have given.

The terribleness of death becomes clear from another vantage point: the perspective of consciousness and of its relation to the world. The experience of life is an experience of consciousness. The mark of consciousness is to present a complete world, not just how I see, feel, and think about myself, but a whole world centered on me, extending outward from my body. For consciousness, everything that exists or that has existed or that will exist exists only because it plays a part in this mental theater of mine. Beyond the perimeter of its stage, there is no world and there is no being.

Continuity of consciousness embodied in an individual human organism is what we mean by a self. The experience of selfhood is the experience of consciousness associated with the fate of the body and is persistent over time until the body fails and dissolves. There are no human beings for whom the world fails to be manifest in this way as extending outward and backward and forward in time from the conscious and embodied self.

We come to learn that this view of the world is an illusion. We correct the illusion (or compensate for it), but only theoretically, that is to say by telling ourselves that the world does not in reality exist in the way in which we will continue to experience it.

Death not only brings the conscious self to an end but also shows, in definitive and incontrovertible form, that the representation of the world as extending outward in space and time from the self was false from the outset. The dead person will not be there to see the demonstration of his error, but the survivors will register what has happened. Each of them will know what awaits.

With the end of consciousness, it is not just the conscious self that disappears forever but also the whole world, as it existed for consciousness, that perishes. The events and protagonists that filled it all vanish suddenly in the instant of death, unless their disappearance has been foreshadowed by the ruin of the mind.

The person may flatter himself that he has recorded his experience of the world in lasting words. We know, however, that such records bear only a distant relation to the flow and richness of conscious life. At best, they select from it or use it, translating it into a language that hardly resembles the real thing. The world of the conscious self cannot escape to the page; it remains trapped in the dying body, which sucks it into the grave and into nothingness.

No afterlife of the kind promised by the religions of salvation can console us for our mortality. An afterlife would not suffice to give us back our bodies; we would need to be given back the time of the historical world, the struggle and the connection with other people in a time that is irreversible and decisive. To be restored to our bodies and made forever young without being reinstated in the time of history would be to suffer the torture of an eternal boredom. For this reason, portrayals of a paradise of eternal life in the salvation religions remain unconvincing and even repellent. They offer us the shell of immortality without granting us what makes life irresistible.

The embodied self is the same person who woke to the world in a burst of visionary immediacy, who soon found that he was not the center of that world but on the contrary a dependent and even hapless creature, and who then discovered that he was doomed to die.

To face death squarely and persistently, without help from the feel-good theologies and philosophies that abound in the history of religion and of metaphysics, is to look straight at a sun that Pascal assured us, with reason, cannot be long observed without danger. It is to live in fear of the incomprehensible and awful end before us.

However, to contrive to forget that we will die – to turn wholly away from death or at least as far away from it as we can – is to risk losing the most powerful antidote to a life of routine, convention, conformity, and submission, to a somnambulant life, which is to say to a life that is not fully possessed and that exhibits only in diminished form the attributes of life: surfeit, spontaneity, and surprise.

It is the prospect of death that gives life its decisive, irreversible shape and makes time – our time – full of weight and consequence. Aroused by the awareness of death, so closely connected to the sentiment of life, we can conceive an existence of striving and can resist the automatisms, the habits, the endless little surrenders that rob us, by installments, of the substance of life.

As we confront this dilemma, we have reason for hope. If we were able to fully awaken to life and to grasp its qualities and possibilities, we might be just as overtaken by a paralyzing sentiment as if we held death firmly in our line of vision. That each of us was snatched out of nothingness before being returned to it (or promoted, according to some of the historical religions, to the perpetual ordeal of an uneventful timelessness) is an enigma of the same order as the riddle of mortality. It is also a fortune so great that it may be as hard to consider steadily as our fall toward death. Life too, seen for what it is or can become, would be a sun blinding us through an exultation that might paradoxically inhibit our ability to seize its benefits.

So we must run back and forth between these two suns in our firmament – the presentiment of death and the awareness of life – and avoid being transfixed by either of them. If we are lucky, we may form attachments and projects that enhance the sentiment of life in this uncertain middle distance. Still, even as we try our luck, death comes to us and brings our experiment to an end.

GROUNDLESSNESS

We are unable to grasp the ground of being – the ultimate basis for our existence in the world and the existence of the world. We cannot look into the beginning and end of time. In our reasoning, one presupposition leads to another and one cause into another. We never reach the bottom: the bottom is bottomless.

The root experience of groundlessness is astonishment that we exist, that the world exists, and that the world and our situation are the way they are rather than another way. Yet, the way they are seems to bear no relation to us other than a great indifference to our concerns. On the concern that overrides all others, however, the attachment to life, nature is not simply indifferent, it is unforgiving. It has condemned each of us to destruction.

Our formulations and understanding of the workings of nature often excludes our core interests. When we do not allow ourselves to be deceived by cowardice, self-deception, wishful thinking, and power worship we discover that there is no basis on which to understand the place and value of our loves and devotions in the history and structure of the universe. Thus, astonishment is accompanied in the core experience of groundlessness by awareness of the incomprehensibility and of the sheer alienness of the world in which we find ourselves.

We face the disorienting implications of the inescapable fact that we play a tiny, marginal part in a story that we did not and would not write. We can edit that story marginally, but we cannot rewrite it. In fact, we can barely understand it, and we survey it only in fragments. Consequently, our decisions about what to do with our brief lives can have no basis outside ourselves. We are ungrounded.

The most salient feature of the world is that it is what it is rather than something else. The most ambitious projects of understanding the world are those that seek to explain why it must be the way it is and could be no other way. They are those that seek to explain why something exists rather than nothing at all. If these endeavors had any merit or prospect of success, our speculative insight into the world might provide a response to our existential groundlessness. They do not.

The world has a history. It extends backward and forward in time, even beyond the present universe. No final system of laws could tell us what this history was or will be or must be; the regularities of nature are the products of this history even more than they are its source. When we come to understand this history much better than we now do, we shall still be confined to play a tiny part in it. It remains foreign to our concerns: its message continues to be that nothing is for keeps and that everything turns into everything else.

What about us? That is the question lying at the heart of the problem of existential groundlessness. A response would make sense of our situation in the world in ways that provide guidance for the conduct of life and for the organization of society. We may first seek outside ourselves a basis for an orientation to existence in our general understanding of the world and of our place in it. If such an understanding yields no clues, we are driven back on ourselves to our biographical and historical experience and on our self-understanding. The question then becomes whether the very lack of a grounding outside ourselves can be turned into an incitement and a justification for our self-grounding.

In every instance, a response to the threat of existential groundlessness must take account of the most frightening aspect of our situation: that we will die. If such a response cannot show us how we are to achieve eternal life, it must suggest at least the beginnings of an approach to how we are to live, given our mortality, our manifest human nature or the human nature that we can bring about, our fundamental needs and desires, and the intractable limits to what we can hope to discover about the world and about our place within it.

Reponses to existential groundlessness

The problem of existential groundlessness can be restated simply: all attempts to ground an orientation to existence in an understanding of the world tend to fail. (To say that they must forever fail would be to make an unjustifiable claim about the future of human insight and initiative.) The previous efforts of religion to manage the threat of existential groundlessness can be succinctly summarized: the better the news, the less reason there is to believe it; the more credible the news, the less satisfactory it is as a response to the perplexities and anxieties motivating the experience of existential groundlessness. There appears to be an adverse sliding scale that places our desire to see things as they against our search for encouragement and guidance. Moreover, even the more credible positions on this sliding scale, which least require us to assent to the unbelievable, are unsatisfactory; if they do not tax our credulity, they nevertheless make light of our powers of resistance and self-transformation.

The most encouraging and least believable news is that we have a friend in charge of the universe. That is the news delivered by the Semitic monotheisms, namely, Judaism, Christianity, and Islam. Our friend made both the world and us out of an abundance of his creative, life-giving love. We are formed in his image. Not satisfied to make us and stand aside, he has a plan for our salvation. According to one version of this narrative, in the implementation of that plan he may even have become incarnate in a man a couple of thousands of years ago. He calls us to eternal life and to participation in his being and requires that we change how we live and deal with one another. A community of the faithful will uphold and spread this good news.

This message is not without its terrors. Our spiritual freedom creates the risk that we may fail to heed the message and follow the path. We may be cut off and suffer estrangement from him. Like our salvation itself, this separation may become irreversible and eternal. Nevertheless, the view that we have a friend in charge of the universe is the best news that we could expect to receive, given our impending death and apparent groundlessness. He is the ground of being and, particularly, of our being. In him, we hope to overcome death.

The trouble is that belief in this narrative may be hard to achieve or to sustain. If it is not simply acquiescence in the conventions of a family and of a culture, it must be the result of undergoing certain experiences. Although these experiences violate our ordinary beliefs about the workings of nature, they may impose themselves on us with compelling if not irresistible force. However, apart from the matter of whether we should allow ourselves to be overwhelmed in this way, we may simply not undergo such experiences. Having undergone them, we may fall out of them.

A second family of responses to our existential groundlessness, of which the teachings of Buddha and the philosophy of the Vedas are the most important examples, emphasizes the impermanence of all the kinds of being through which nature momentarily presents itself and therefore of all the regular relations among these types of beings as well. Under the changing disguises of nature it discerns changeless and unified being. This radical impermanence suggests that not only is all phenomenal distinction illusory, including distinction among selves, but that time itself is only "the moving image of eternity." Our sole reliable grounding, according to this view, is the one that enables us to disentangle ourselves through insight and striving from the coils of the phenomenal world and to increase our participation in the underlying one reality – the reality of being. Such is also the route to an inclusive compassion, seeing beyond the shallow and ephemeral divisions among us and within the world. Death confirms, with respect to our embodied existence, the truth of impermanence. It signals our return to the ground of being, from which we never truly departed.

Here is news that is not as good as the news about our friend the creator and master of the universe and his plan to rescue us from death and groundlessness. If time is illusory, so is history, and our worldly engagements turn out to be either paths without goals or goals without paths. To accept this way of dealing with our existential groundlessness, we would have to begin by denying or by devaluing the reality of the manifest world and of time. It is one thing to affirm the thesis of impermanence. It is another to diminish the reality of the impermanent so long as it exists. It is in this respect that the news is incredible.

A third approach to our existential groundlessness is illustrated by the teachings of Confucius, as well as by many strands in Western secular humanism. It begins from a wholly different point of departure. It proposes that we ground ourselves by building a culture and a society bearing the mark of our concerns and fostering our better selves. The great spectacle of nature is meaningless, according to this view. We can hope to master a small part of it and to make it serve our interests; we cannot, however, bridge the chasm between the vast indifference of the cosmos and the requirements of humanity. All that we can do is to create a meaningful order within an otherwise meaningless cosmos. Our best chance of establishing such an order is to refine who we are and how we deal with one another. We can do so through a dialectic between the rules, roles, and rituals of society and the gradual strengthening of our powers of imaginative empathy – our ability to understand the experience of other people and to minister to their needs. By performing our obligations to one another, as chiefly defined by the roles we perform in society, we can secure the humanized structure that nature denies us.

This view makes two mistakes that compromise its prospect of disposing of the problem of existential groundlessness, a mistake about society and history and a mistake about the self. The mistake about society and history is to credit any particular social regime with the power to accommodate all the experiences that we have reason to value or to represent the authoritative setting for the discharge of our obligations to one another. Because no social regime can be incontestable, none can hope to provide a grounding for human life that could make up for the grounding that nature denies us.

The mistake about the self is to depreciate a truth about humanity that is revealed in the third irreparable flaw in the human condition (which I next discuss): our insatiability. We demand of one another, as well as of the social and cultural worlds that we build and inhabit, more than we and they can offer. The advancement of our most fundamental material and moral interests regularly requires us to defy and to revise any settled plan of social life. The ultimate source of this power of resistance and defiance is that there is more in us, individually as well as collectively, than there is, or ever can be, in such regimes. We depend on others to make a self. At the same time, we fear dependence as subjugation. Here the making and the undoing of the self have similar sources.

The provisional conclusion is that none of the ways in which the major civilizations of world history have addressed existential groundlessness succeed. They are defective as theory only because they are also defective as practice. Their practical consequences reveal their theoretical deficiencies.

We must die without grasping reasons for our existence

The combination of our mortality with our groundlessness imparts to human life its pressing and enigmatic character. We struggle in our brief time in the midst of an impenetrable darkness. A small area is lit up: our civilizations, our sciences, our works, our loves. We prove unable to deny the place of the lighted area within a larger space devoid of light and must go to our deaths unenlightened.

A central issue in the history of religion is whether it will remain content to perform the role of providing the consolation that we desire. A subsequent issue is what we are entitled to hope for if we cannot rest assured in the expectations that those consoling beliefs hold out for us. Both issues form major concerns of the argument of this book.

We must die without grasping reasons for our existence other than those fragments of necessity and chance that scientific inquiry suggests to us. It does not seem that the growth of scientific knowledge ever would or could alter this circumstance. If there is one universe or many, if the universe is eternal or time-bound, if it had a beginning in time or began together with time, we would simply have different ways of expressing a riddle that we would remain powerless to solve.

INSATIABILITY

Insatiability is a third incurable defect in human life. Our desires are insatiable. We seek from the limited the unlimited. Yet here we must fail. Our insatiability is rooted in our natural constitution. Human desires are indeterminate. They fail to exhibit the targeted and scripted quality of desire among other animals. Even when, as in addiction and obsession, they fix on particular objects, we make those particular objects serve as proxies for longings to which they have a loose or arbitrary relation. We force the limited to serve as a surrogate for the unlimited. This misalliance, revealed most starkly in our obsessional and addictive behavior, carries over to our entire experience of wanting and seeking.

The retreat or vagueness of biological determination in the shaping of our desires opens space for the working of four forces that together make our desires insatiable.

A first root of insatiability is the imprinting of the dialectic of embodiment and transcendence on the life of desire. We suffer when desire goes unsatisfied; when it is satisfied we are briefly relieved of pain. Our desires, however, are unlimited in both their number and their reach. The moment of dissatisfaction is soon followed by other unrequited wants. Contentment remains a momentary interlude in an experience of privation and longing that has no end. How could it be different? No narrowly directed set of desires defines our natures. Hence no particular satisfactions can leave us lastingly at ease. The problem with the particular desires and the particular satisfactions is that they are particular and that we are not.

A second root of insatiability is the social construction of desire. Our desires lack a predetermined content. To a large extent, we get the content from one another; our desires represent a kidnapping of the self by society. This commandeering of desire by other people makes the content of desire seem empty, as if it always remained on the periphery of the self, as if it never penetrated the inner and empty core of the personality. We stand forever ready to exchange one invasion of the self by society for another.

A third root of insatiability is the prominence of those desires that can never be satisfied. We want from one another acceptance, recognition, and admiration, as well as things and power. In particular, we want from one another what every child wants from every parent: an assurance that there is an unconditional place for him the world. No such assurance is ever enough, because every assurance is both ambiguous and revocable. What is given to one person is taken from another, so that we find ourselves in a circumstance of perpetual dissatisfaction. Only love, freely given but easily destroyed, could free us for a while from this endless yearning.

A fourth root of insatiability is that we seek not just to rid ourselves of the pains and privations but also to supply a response to both death and groundlessness. A person may seek to become rich because he cannot become immortal or because he cannot find any more reliable grounding for his existence. This ceaseless metonymy, this trading of the ultimate for the homely, is bound to disappoint him.

There is a common element in these sources of insatiability. We cannot access the absolute, the unconditional, the unlimited. Therefore, we try to get it from the limited. We are unable to convince ourselves that, despite our mortality and our groundlessness, everything is all right. Therefore, we use whatever material and immaterial resources we can obtain to compensate for the fundamental defects in life that we are powerless to redress. We can never achieve enough acceptance from one another. Therefore, each of us continues the hunt for more tokens of assurance that there is an unconditional place for him in the world. We cannot restrict our strivings to a limited set of objects and goals. Therefore, we walk a treadmill of desire, satisfaction, boredom, and new desire, and take from others the cues that we are never adequately able to give ourselves.

The result is exposure to a free-floating anguish that it has been the aim of much of religion, philosophy, and art to quiet. Speculative thought and religious practice enlisted in the cause of self-help have often served as devices by which we cast a spell on ourselves the better to free ourselves from the sufferings of insatiability. From them we garner the stories about the cosmos and our lives within it that make the spell seem to be a reception of the deepest truths about the world.

The emptiness of human desires

At the center of the experience of insatiability lies the emptiness of human desires. That is, their indeterminacy in comparison to the desires of other animals. This negativity influences even those drives for food and sex that most clearly tie us to the rest of the animal world but that in the human being have an unfixed, inclusive, and roaming quality. This emptiness of desire appears under two main aspects: it is mimetic (to use René Girard's term) and it is projected (to use Karl Rahner's term). The preceding discussion has already suggested how each of these traits of desire plays a part in the genealogy of insatiable desire. Together, they help clarify the nature of our insatiability.

Because our desires are empty, the void will be filled up by other people. To a large extent we desire what those around us desire. Their desires contaminate us; they take us over. This take-over establishes a basis for both competition and cooperation, according to both the content of what is desired and the range of social alternatives available for its pursuit.

If we failed to resist the imitative character of desire even as we surrender to it, we would not be the individuals who we are. We would not be the beings whose relations to one another are shadowed by an inescapable ambivalence because they seek connection without subjugation and who understand, however darkly, that "imitation is suicide." There is no making of selves without connection in every domain of our existence, and there is no connection in any realm of experience without the risk of loss of self. "Accept me but make me free" is what every human being says to another.

This conflicted relation both to the others and to the organized contexts of life and of thought takes place in the midst of a struggle for the fulfillment of our desires, desires that we discover to be not really ours. They come to us largely from the influence of others. Unless we can somehow criticize these borrowed desires, change them, and make them ours, our ambivalence to other people and our resistance to the context are powerless to free and to empower us. Therefore it is not only to other people that we are ambivalent but also to our own desires, because they are ours and not ours. This confusion enters into the experience of insatiability and endows it with its tortured and desperate quality.

It is widely believed that these complications are the result of a historically specific set of developments in society and culture associated with the ascendancy of democratic, liberal, and romantic ideals. The truth however is closer to being the opposite: it is the power of these fundamental experiences of the self, which no regime of society and culture can entirely override or suppress that accounts for the irresistible seductions of these forms of life and consciousness. The prophetic voice in politics and in culture would fall on deaf ears if it failed to find an ally in the innermost recesses of the self.

In addition to this mimesis, desire is also projected, and it is projected in a twofold sense. On the one hand, it always yearns for something beyond its immediate and manifest object. This "something beyond" shares in the quality of the unlimited, the unconditional, the absolute, the infinite. Thus, desire is projected in the sense that it projects forward beyond its visible horizon. On the other hand, however, the something beyond remains remote and obscure. We approach it almost always by indirection, mistaking it for something tangible and accessible, the proximate and visible object of our longing. Thus, desire is projected in the sense that we project the hidden absolute onto a manifest, contingent, and all-too-particular object.

In obsession and addiction, the disproportionate and even capricious bond between the hidden horizon of the unlimited and the paltry surrogate for it becomes extreme and paradoxical. It is however only the limiting case of a pervasive feature of the life of desire. In boredom we experience directly the failure of the particular objects of desire and of the habits and routines surrounding their pursuit to hold our interest by engaging our capabilities. In every quarter, the phenomenology of desire bears the mark of our insatiability and reveals its connection with our powers of transcendence, with our longing for the infinite.

The projected quality of desire shows how our insatiability relates to our mortality and our groundlessness. The brevity of life lends urgency to the pursuits of desire: our time will end while we continue to seek one unworthy object after another, each the proxy for the unreachable horizon of that which could satisfy us. The terrors of death grow in the imagination with the expenditure of life on this equivocal chase. Our uncertainty about the grounding of our existence (or rather the failure of all the available proposals to ground it) leaves us without a route by which to go from the tangible and defective particulars that we can grasp to the intangible and indiscriminate absolute that we voicelessly seek.

Love and work

Variations of society and culture cannot save us from our insatiability, but can some of our initiatives as individuals nevertheless shield us against it? Can we not have in love and in work experiences that wholly absorb us – modifying or even suspending our sense of the passage of time – without depriving us of consciousness and thereby interrupt the cycle of unrequited desire?

Yes, if we are both lucky and wise, but only for a while. The work will come to an end and no longer represent for its creator what it represented in the throes of creation. The love ever tainted by ambivalence will cease to waver only if it ceases to live. The work and the love will be revealed as a particular engagement and a particular connection, and we will continue to seek absurdly and inescapably something that is not merely one more particular. In this way, our reprieves from insatiable desire are momentary; our insatiability remains as the lasting undercurrent of our experience, thrown into starker relief by its remissions.

Insofar as we are death-bound, existence is urgent and frightful. Insofar as we are groundless, it is vertiginous and dreamlike. Insofar as we are insatiable, it is unquiet and tormented.

BELITTLEMENT

The poet William Wordsworth once said that the true sorrow of humanity consists in this: not that the minds of humans fail, but that the course and the demands of action and of life so rarely correspond with the dignity and intensity of human desires. This understanding describes what we may be tempted to mistake for a fourth irreparable flaw in the human condition: belittlement.

No feature of our humanity is more important than our power to go beyond the particular regimes of society and of thought in which we participate. We can always do, feel, think, or create more than our societies will bless, allow, or make sense of. The fecundity and amplitude of experience outreach all the formative limitations imposed. For the same reasons and in the same sense, no social role in any society can do justice to any individual human being. No scheme of social organization can accommodate all the activities that we have reason to value or all the powers that we have cause to exercise and to develop. This excess over the determinate circumstances of existence should excite in the mind the idea of our greatness or of our share in the attributes that some of the world religions have ascribed to God.

Nevertheless, the ordinary experience of life, although punctuated by moments of joy that may be sustained and prolonged by our engagements and attachments, is one of blockage and humiliation. The persistent disproportion between our context-transcending powers and the objects on which we lavish our devotions threatens to turn existence into an ordeal of belittlement. "In every house, in the heart of each maiden, and of each boy, in the soul of the soaring saint, this chasm is found," wrote Emerson. "[It is found] between the largest promise of ideal power, and the shabby experience...So each man is an emperor deserted by his states, and left to whistle by himself." The extremes of economic deprivation and social oppression to which most of humankind has been condemned for most of history make this ordeal seem all the more bitter and inescapable. If we look beyond the surface of life, however, we see that not even the privileged, the powerful, the gifted, and the lucky are free from the burdens of belittlement. These burdens result universally from the recurrent, shaping incidents of a human life.

Even a person whose circumstances and fortune have shielded him from deprivation and oppression must face these trials in three successive waves in the course of his existence. First, at the beginning, he must be driven out of the sense that he is the eternal center of the world – he must come to understand not only that he is just one among countless many but also that he will soon be nothing. Later he must resign himself to taking a particular course in life, if indeed the course is not imposed on him by the constraints of society. However, the consequence of the particularity of the course of life is to open a rift between who we are and how we must live. The individual knows himself darkly to be more, much more than his outward existence reveals. He faces the burdens of belittlement a third time as he grows older and settles into an existence that he has embraced, or that has been forced upon him. A carapace of routine, of compromise, of silent surrenders, of half-term solutions, and of diminished consciousness begins to form around him. He begins to die small deaths, many times over. This third encounter with belittlement reveals belittlement for what it in fact is: death by installments.

Just what we can and should do about our susceptibility to belittlement as individuals and as societies is crucial to the course of life and to the advance of humanity. Our struggle with the threat of belittlement can easily be misdirected. One such false direction seeks to avoid or overcome belittlement by holding before us false hope of escaping our mortality, our groundlessness, or our insatiability. Another mistaken path accepts a particular established, or proposed, regime of society or of thought as the definitive template for our triumph over belittlement. The most important disorientation of all fails to see how the conduct of life may preserve us from the evils of belittlement, so long as we are not overwhelmed by the frailties of the body and the cruelties of society. It regards belittlement as no more avoidable than death.

What to do about our susceptibility to belittlement has always been a theme in the religious consciousness of humanity. For the more than twenty-five hundred years that witnessed the emergence, spread, and influence of the present world religions, it has, however, remained largely a subterranean theme. An argument of this book is that it should now become a central and guiding concern.

Generic antidotes to belittlement: Collective and individual

The generic antidote to belittlement is empowerment, collective or individual. There are principal false forms of individual and collective empowerment, which now exercise commanding influence. They are not false in the sense that they fail to increase the power of the species or of the individual. They are false in the sense that despite their contribution to our empowerment, they cannot keep their promises; they fail to repair our susceptibility to belittlement as it is faced by each man and woman in the course of life. I call the chief false collective remedy the romance of the ascent of humanity, and the chief false individual remedy Prometheanism.

In the romance of our ascent, humanity rises. Its rise is not inevitable – not at least in the more guarded and realistic versions of the romance of ascent – but it is possible. (Auguste Comte and Karl Marx, two philosophers of this romance, were not so circumspect.) We the human race have already gone far to diminish our haplessness before nature. When we depended completely on nature, we worshiped nature. Now we have built great civilizations. We have formed, through science and technology, instruments with which to extend our powers and to prolong our lives. We have created opportunities for many more people to have more time to explore the secrets of the universe as well as the workings of society and of the mind. All these achievements are only a beginning. The watchword of the romance of the ascent of humanity is the following: you have not seen anything yet.

This romance of ascent supplies a response to our trials of belittlement that is inadequate in two distinct ways. In the first instance, it is inadequate because, unless the individual can share in his own lifetime in this rise, he casts himself in the role of instrument of the species, as if we were ants rather than human beings. We allow biographical time to vanish within historical time, or make it figure only as a period of servitude, even when our indenture is voluntary. We become estranged from the supreme good – the only good that we ever really possess: life in the present. Augustine said that all epochs are equidistant from eternity. What are we to tell the individual who, in a scheme like that of Comte or of Marx, happens to have been born far before the consummation of history? That the miseries of slave society or of the capitalist sweatshop were necessary to the emancipation of an unborn humanity? The positive social theorist or the philosopher of history who believes that he has uncovered the hidden script of historical necessity may profess no interest in such an anxiety. The individual, however, who has resorted to the ascent of humanity as a response to the trials of belittlement must ask himself how the future empowerment of the species makes up for his present subjection. If he has come to understand that history has no such script and that, although the future rise of the race is possible, it is neither inevitable in its occurrence nor foreordained in its content, then his dissatisfaction will be all the greater.

In the second instance, the romance of the ascent of humankind is inadequate as a solution to the problem of our susceptibility to belittlement because its true and hidden attraction comes from another, largely unacknowledged quarter. Under cover of being a response to belittlement, it is in fact also an answer to death. If we cannot bring ourselves to believe the metaphysic (which I call in this book the overcoming of the world) according to which the distinct existence of the self is less real than the unified and timeless being from which all emanates and to which all returns, we can nevertheless persuade ourselves to accept a weaker version of that doctrine. According to this version, we are indeed the real individuals that we seem to be, living in a historical world that is also for real. We shall have to accept death and the dissolution of the body to which consciousness remains tied. We shall nevertheless survive in the onward rush of emergent humanity. I, the individual, however, will not survive. The future glories of the human race will not elate me now, nor will its future absurdities and savageries cast me down. Each of us can work out of love or ambition for the unborn. Only a fool bent on consolation would find in our sacrifice the rescue from death.

Once the specter of this secondhand immortality vanishes, the romance of the ascent of the human race loses much of its luster. It loses it not only as a compensation for death but also as a cure for belittlement. What we do must make us greater now, even at the price of abruptly shortening the life in which this greatness is manifest. All true greatness may be sacrificial. As the beneficiaries of sacrifice, however, those who have yet to live enjoy no priority over the living.

Prometheanism

Prometheanism is what I call the most influential individualist response to the evil of belittlement. At its core is the idea that the individual can raise himself beyond the plane of ordinary existence where the mass of ordinary men and women allow themselves to be diminished. He can do so by becoming the radical original that he already inchoately is and by turning his life into a work of art. To say that he turns his life into a work of art is to affirm that he raises it to a level of power and radiance at which it becomes a source of values rather than a continual exercise of conformity to values that are imposed on him by the conventions and preconceptions of society. It is a position that was given voice by Nietzsche more than by any other thinker. Rousseau and Emerson approached it but never surrendered to it.

Prometheanism beats the drum in the face of death. Here the individual exults in his powers and above all in his power to fashion himself and to become a creator of value. But the individual fails to achieve literal deathlessness and remains condemned to the annihilation of the body and of consciousness. Nevertheless, he may hope to achieve the next best thing to immortality: he lives among men and women who remain below on a lower rung of the ladder of existential ascent as if he were one of the immortal gods. The clearest sign of this election – in truth, a self-election or a self-crowning – is change in the experience of time. It is our absorption in activities that, without denying our mortality and finitude, suspend for us the oppressive passage of time. Thus, we have a taste of eternity without leaving our mortal bodies.

I name this view Prometheanism by poetic license, for in so calling it I do injustice to Prometheus, who stole fire from heaven to give it to humanity. These Prometheans steal fire to give it to themselves.

The overt defect of Prometheanism is its denial of the claims of solidarity in the making of the self. No person makes himself or herself. We are made by the grace of others – through connection with them in every realm of existence. Because every connection threatens us with loss of freedom and of distinction, even as it may give us the self that we have or can develop, our dealings with others are fraught with an inescapable ambivalence, the other side of the mimetic character of desire. The idea that the triumph of the individual over belittlement must take place against the backdrop of a distinction between a small number who become artificers of their own lives and creators of value and a hapless mass that sinks back into conformity and enslavement entangles the winners as well as the losers – the powerful as well as the powerless – in anxious vigilance to uphold or to undermine the arrangements of this dominion.

The greatest and most fundamental mistake of Prometheanism is its hidden program: to overwhelm through power and power worship – through the raising up of the strong self over the weak herd – the irremediable defects in our existence, death first among them. The stated antidote to death is a surge of creation. The objects of creation are the elements of such an inner-directed and self-grounded form of life. The aim is to act as if we were not the hapless and inconsolable creatures that we seem to be. It is acceleration and empowerment in the face of an imminent dissolution. It is to fill existence with activities that make time stop.

The cure for insatiability, according to the Promethean, is to direct desire inward to ourselves. Only the infinite self, towering over circumstance can quench our desire for the absolute, which the believer sought mistakenly in the love of a God who was only the alienated projection of his own self. By such a projection, the believer leaves enslaved what the Promethean proposes to unchain.

The remedy for groundlessness is to ground oneself through successive acts of creation of a form of life for the design of which no human need apply to his fellows. From this self-grounding, forms, values, and practices will result, cleansed of conformity to the social regime. How is this self-creator to know what to create? He will discover himself through non-conformity to his society and resistance to his time. Having discovered himself, he will become himself by that same struggle.

Prometheanism fails above all because it lies to us about the human condition. Like the religions that it despises, it is a lullaby, a feel-good story and an effort to arouse the will in its confrontation with circumstances that the will is unable to alter. The cost of this self deception is to undermine the very good of life that it affects to prize. It does so by discrediting the context-bound engagements and attachments on which the quickening and heightening of life depend. It does so as well by treating truth – the truth about our situation in the world – as subsidiary to power. The fables to which Prometheanism resorts misrepresent our existence, and thus they cannot guide us in the enhancement of life.

It is the irreparable flaws in existence that help give our lives their shape and potential. It is their terrors that awaken us from the slumber of conformity and bring us to the encounter with time. In turning away from them, we make the mistake of supposing that we can become more godlike by becoming less human.

Like the romance of the ascent of humanity, Prometheanism is a falsehood that resembles a truth. It is a dead end easily mistaken for a path. The falsehood is power worship, the subordination of solidarity to self-reliance, and the failure fully to recognize and to accept the incurable defects in the human condition. The truth is that the enhancement of life is our chief interest; the enhancement of life is central to what I here call the religion of the future.

RELIGION AND THE FLAWS OF HUMAN EXISTENCE

With respect to these flaws in the basic circumstance of existence, everything will never be all right. A religion offering us no assurance that everything is all right would differ from what religion has been in history. It would amount to a third moment in the history of our spiritual experience. The major spiritual orientations to the world, prominent over the last two and a half thousand years, assure us that everything will indeed be all right. We shall be able to redress the flaws in our existence – our mortality, our groundlessness, our insatiability, and our susceptibility to belittlement – or, at least, to rob them of their terrors. Without some such faith, it may seem, life, our life, would remain both an enigma and a torment, and could cease to be a torment only insofar as we contrived to forget the enigma. Nothing could attenuate the sufferings of these wounds other than our connections and engagements and our absorption in life.

The trouble is that the antidotes supplied by the historical religions may all be fanciful, wishful thinking dressed up as a view of the world and of our place within it, consolation in place of truth. The religion of the future should be one that dispenses with consolation. It should nevertheless offer a response to the defective character of our existence, not just a set of ideas but an orientation to the life of the individual and the history of society. It should show us what we can hope for once we have lost the beliefs in which we once found reassurance. The disposition to acknowledge our situation for what it is would signal a change in the history of religion.

In the following chapter I explore the internal architecture of the major spiritual options – overcoming the world, humanizing the world, and struggling with the world. I do so with the intention of going beyond them, not with the aim of making claims about the distinctive doctrines and singular histories of the particular religions that have expressed them. Here, the historical allusions remain ancillary to a philosophical and theological argument. The argument is chiefly concerned with the choice of a direction. I call this direction the religion of the future.

CHAPTER 2

Three Orientations to Existence

THE ARGUMENT DEVELOPED in this book takes as its point of departure an analysis of the previous responses to the flaws in our existence. It identifies three key orientations in the history of humanity, which took shape in the thousand-year period extending from before the second half of the first millennium before Christ to after the first half of the first millennium after Christ. I call these orientations overcoming the world, humanizing the world, and struggling with the world.

This chapter outlines each of the orientations followed by detailed criticism. Having laid out their programs and shortcomings I then identify five common characteristics of the religions of these orientations, despite their differences: a rejection of cosmotheism, anti-nihilism, an emphasis on unity, attack on authority, and ambiguity to state power. All five of these commonalities were marked by an ambiguity, the resolution of which helps define the agenda of a religious revolution of the future.

OVERCOMING THE WORLD

Central idea, historical presence, and metaphysical vision

The vision of the world embraced by this first direction in the religious history of humanity is one that has always been exceptional in Western philosophy since the time of the Greeks. It has, however, also been predominant in many other civilizations. It is the position to which philosophy and religion have most often returned outside of the West.

The Indic Vedanta, the Upanishads, early Buddhism, and early Daoism represent the clearest instances of this religious and philosophical path. In these traditions, it has had any number of metaphysical elaborations; for example, Nagarjuna's doctrine of emptiness (sunyata) in the context of the Madhyamaka school of Indian Buddhism. It describes aspects of the doctrines of Parmenides, Plato, the Stoics, and the Neoplatonists, especially Plotinus. In modern Western thought, the teaching of Schopenhauer is its consummate expression, both as metaphysics and as practical philosophy. We can also find it under different cover in both the monism of Spinoza and the relationalism of Leibniz, the decisive common element of which is the denial of the ultimate reality of time and a rejection of the distinctions among the time-drenched and seemingly mutable phenomena for which we mistake as real.

The overcoming of the world resonates in the mystical countercurrents of Judaism, Christianity, and Islam. In Jewish, Christian, and Muslim mysticism, the opening to a personal God risks being sacrificed to a vision of impersonal, unified, and universal being. This vision in turn inspires an ethic of selfless benevolence and a quest for indifference to suffering and change. It does so, however, on the basis of a devaluation of the reality of time and of the distinctions among beings, including the distinction among selves. No wonder these mystics have regularly fallen under the suspicion of heresy in each of the Semitic monotheisms.

The metaphysical idea informing this approach to existence is the affirmation of universal being lying behind the manifest world of time, distinction, and individuality. The philosophy and theology of the overcoming of the world tell us that time, distinction, and individuality are unreal or that they are less real than they seem to be. The metaphysic of the overcoming of the world affirms the ephemeral character of all distinctions among types of being at the same time that it denies the reality of time.

The theoretical answer to the fear that our lives and the world itself may be meaningless is to cast aside the beliefs, the attachments, and the engagements that prevent us from recognizing our participation in timeless and universal being. The overcoming of the world thus becomes an overcoming of the will, the development of an attitude to the world that is will-less. The dismissal of time, distinction, and individual selfhood and the supersession of the will are thus the two fixed and central points in this metaphysical conception. The campaign against the will in turn serves as a bridge connecting this metaphysical view to the ideals of serenity through invulnerability and of detached, universal benevolence that are characteristic of this approach to life.

Serenity and benevolence

These ideas and incitements inspire a vision of how to live. In that vision, the two central commitments are to serenity and benevolence, which are closely linked.

We achieve serenity by conquering the will. We cultivate an inner reserve from the commotions of this shadowy domain, a reserve founded upon our acknowledgment of the truth – of the One being or of the archetypes of reality – lying behind the veil of time, distinction, and individual selfhood. We discount the significance of the ups and downs of worldly fortune. We become, to that extent, invulnerable; invulnerability and serenity represent two aspects of this same ideal of existence. We experience, right now, our share in the hidden reality of the One or in the hidden realities of the models of being.

A disinterested and universal benevolence forms alongside this ideal of serenity and self-possession. Its distinctive tone is sacrificial attentiveness to the needs of others, marked by distance and detachment. Such benevolence is highest and purest when not compromised by any erotic interest or by any proximity of blood, community, or common interest. It is best experienced and offered by a person who has already triumphed over the illusions of the will.

The metaphysical basis of this ideal of benevolence is the same as the metaphysical foundation of the ideal of serenity. It is the acknowledgment of the falsehood or shallowness of all the divisions within the cosmos as well as within humankind. The overcoming of the world infers the denial or devaluation of the barriers within humanity – a shared theme of the religions of transcendence – from its most general thesis about the ultimately real. The practical consequence for the ideal of benevolence is that our sacrificial good will should reach out not just to other human beings and to nonhuman sentient creatures but even, as well, to all beings caught in the toils of illusory distinction and change.

From this understanding of serenity and benevolence results a response to death, groundlessness, insatiability, and belittlement.

The overcomers of the world and of the will deny death by affirming that the life of the individual self was to begin with an illusory or derivative phenomenon. In the radical versions of the metaphysic of overcoming, the dissolution of the body breaks down the barrier that sustained the illusion of our estrangement from one and timeless being. In the qualified versions, death represents an incident in an itinerary (for example, of the transmigration of the soul, to be embodied in other individual organisms) that has our reunion with one and timeless being as its goal.

The overcomers deny groundlessness by moving toward what they regard to be the ground of existence, concealed from us by the phantasms of our mendacious experience of time, distinction, and individual selfhood. Communion with that ground is the ultimate source of both insight and happiness. It is the sole trustworthy guarantee of the serenity that we should seek and of the benevolence that we should practice.

The overcomers deny insatiability by professing to teach us the only way in which we can free ourselves from insatiable desire: turning aside from the source of desire in the unquiet and embodied self. By negating both the seat and the target of desire and by dismissing or devaluing the impermanent, we escape the ordeal of insatiability. Our escape begins in the right understanding of the world and in the pursuit on the basis of such understanding of the ideals of serenity and of benevolence.

The overcomers deny the inescapability of belittlement by affirming our connection to the source of all reality and value, which is one and timeless being. The phenomena separating us from the real and the valuable, they claim, can also become the bridge to the hidden truth of our being if we understand them correctly and act according to this insight. By crossing this bridge, they hold, we can experience divinity now.

Criticism: betrayal of the past

The forms of belief and of conduct characteristic of this religious orientation respond to the common and fundamental concerns of the past religious revolutions; most notably, the tearing down of the barriers within humanity and the supersession of the ethic of the strong and their lordship over the weak. Although they address these aims and hold out the tantalizing prospect of satisfying them, they cannot in fact achieve them. The fundamental reason for this inadequacy is simple: we cannot change the world or ourselves by standing and waiting: We can do so only by acting.

The trouble is that this orientation pushes adherents in contradictory directions. The effort to enact the vision through a reshaping of social relations inspired by the ideal of a world-embracing sympathy is undermined by the view of ultimate reality that informs it. The orientation affirms the deep unity of suffering humanity and all living creatures; in contesting the boundaries of the self it advocates benevolent action in universal selfhood. However, in denying or diminishing the significance of what goes on in both the historical time of societies and the biographical time of individuals, it undermines the reasons for transformative action. It takes humanity to the threshold of struggle with the world and leaves men and women there with an emotion but without a program.

Criticism: the school of experience

Now consider this approach to existence by the standard of its psychological reality and stability – its connection with our most deep-seated dispositions. Viewed from this perspective, its flaw is its war against life, life as it really is, manifest in the living individual and the mortal organism.

The denial of the reality of the individual self is a denial of death. It is also an anticipation of death, as if we could rob death of its terrors by foreshadowing right now the dissolution of the self into universal mind. Death is denied by a series of connected, self-fulfilling prophecies that are to free us from the cares and distractions of mortality and to put us in communion with a reality that the decay of our mortal bodies cannot corrupt.

Life, however, fights back. We cannot protect ourselves in this way against death without diminishing or devaluing our dealings with the world and with the people around us, which is to say, without suppressing life. It is as if the way to redress the irremediable flaws in our existence were to have less existence. We transport ourselves out of the coils of our alienated existence into a universal experience without the dangerous boundaries of embodiment and time in which we seem to find ourselves encased.

The followers of the overcoming of the world will deny that they wage a war against life. They will claim that their road to salvation enables us to get off the treadmill of insatiable and frustrated desire and allows us to live in the present, open to the world and to the people around us. If each moment and each experience are to be valued as steps to what could or should succeed them, then we shall never live for now. We shall postpone the fuller possession of life. Our anxious striving will make us less receptive to the people as well as the phenomena within reach.

These moves turn us away from the engagements required for the enhancement of life. The orientation promises serenity but delivers a foretaste of death. In tempting us to don a coat of armor against the sufferings induced by our mortality, our groundlessness, our insatiability, and our difficulty in living as beings who transcend their contexts, it cannot in fact make us more receptive to the people and to the phenomena surrounding us, for it denies us the means and the occasions by which to imagine them. It fails to strengthen the sentiment of life within us because it prefers serenity to vitality.

Criticism: betrayal of the future

The religions of the overcoming of the world were never capable of carrying out the shared element in the program of past religious revolution. Moreover, they could never be reconciled to the tenacious dispositions and aspirations of humanity except through a deliberate dimming of consciousness and vitality undertaken in the futile quest to achieve serenity through invulnerability. Similarly, they cannot serve as a starting point for a future revolution in the religious affairs of humankind that is animated by the aim of lifting humanity up, of enhancing our powers, of intensifying our experience, of giving us a wider share in the attributes of divinity, of acting on the principle that we can become better servants of one another if we become greater masters of the structures of society and of thought to which we habitually surrender our humanity.

The overcoming of the world is an adversary of such a revolution by virtue both of how it asks us to understand our situation and of how it calls us to act. The orientation discourages us from engaging in the successive confrontations with society, culture, and ourselves that are required to advance this undertaking. The call takes us in a direction that is opposite to the one we must pursue to achieve the needed religious revolution. It does so at the very outset of its proposals to the self by teaching the individual to raise a shield against suffering and change when her first task is to cast her shield down.

HUMANIZING THE WORLD

Central idea, historical presence, and metaphysical vision

I first provide a sketch of the humanization of the world as a long-standing option within the religious history of humanity. I do so of its core beliefs and without regard to the varieties and specificities of its evolution. The natural world, according to this orientation, is indifferent to humankind and largely impenetrable to the mind. It is inhuman and vastly disproportionate to us. Unable to peer into the beginning or the end of time or to measure the outer limits or hidden depths of reality, we remain confined to explaining parts of the world without ever being able to grasp the relation of the part over which we cast light to the indefinitely larger part that stays unseen. We flatter ourselves in vain that our more or less successful ways of explaining pieces of nature will enable us to explain nature as a whole, when, in fact, the whole remains eternally beyond our reach.

The world is meaningless, according to this orientation. Its meaninglessness lies in our inability to make sense of reality and history in terms pertinent to human concerns: our commitments, attachments, and engagements. If the world is meaningless, so is our place within it. Will this larger meaninglessness overshadow all that we are able to experience and accomplish within our human realm, or shall we succeed in preventing the meaninglessness of the world from undermining our ability to ground ourselves?

We can step back from the edge of the abyss, however, this orientation asserts, and build a human realm. In this realm, human beings create meaning, albeit in a meaningless world. The power and authority of their production of light can be all the greater by virtue of contrast to the surrounding darkness and of the consequent urgency and value of the saving intervention. Only in this way can we rescue ourselves from the absurdity of our condition.

The aim of this orientation is to ensure that society not be contaminated by the meaninglessness of the world, that it not operate under the sway of forces and according to standards that make life among our fellows almost as alien to our deepest concerns as is nature to the shared experience of humanity. If this inner line of defense fails, all is lost. If we can hold the enemy of life-shadowing meaninglessness at bay, in the zone between an indefensible outer line and an indispensable inner line, we can go forward. We have reason to hope.

The overriding goal is to reshape our relations to other people according to a vision of what we owe one another by virtue of occupying certain roles: friend and friend, husband and wife, parent and child, teacher and student, ruler and ruled, boss and worker. In this saving exercise, we shall be guided not only by the practical imperatives of the division of labor in society but also and above all by a sense of the relativity of these roles with respect to our common humanity.

Fate has cast us in different roles. The centrality of roles to the organization of society reveals our dependence on one another. This dependence is a mark rather than a denial of our humanity. It reveals our strength as well as our weakness. Cooperation organized through the performance of roles and the observance of social conventions is not only a requirement for the advancement of our practical interests but also an expression of a basic fact about our humanity: incomplete in ourselves, we complete ourselves through service to others. To serve them, we must understand them. Thus, the development of our imagination of the otherness of other people – the perception of their states of consciousness – forms part of the process by which we complete ourselves, affirming and developing our humanity. Such imagination must inform our performance of social roles.

What is sacrosanct is the person, together with the fine texture of relations among individuals. All else in society and culture remains subservient to the experience of personality and of personal encounter. In a meaningless world, only personality and the relations among persons are hallowed. We should recognize one another as instances of the sacred; that is to say, of that which can create meaning. Everything else in society is a means to an end.

In conformity to this aim and in the service of this goal, the division of labor in society must be softened and spiritualized. It must become the vehicle of our role-based practices of cooperation and of our slowly developing capacity to imagine one another. Our cooperative practices, anchored in the performance of social roles, must be both accommodated and spiritualized according to the demands and the resources of each historical circumstance. Ravenous self-interest must be mastered in the interest of such a humanization of social life. Some element of hierarchy may be admitted, but only so long as it can be justified by the practical requirements of coordination (rather than by belief in the intrinsic qualities of different classes and castes). Only to the extent that we reform society in this way can we prevent its fall into a nightmare of domination and tame our selfishness.

The most comprehensive and influential example of this orientation is the teaching of Confucius as presented in the *Analects*. The subsequent tradition of neo-Confucianism often departed from this tradition by trying to ground the reformation of society in a metaphysical view of the cosmos. In this respect, the latter resembled the Hellenistic philosophies that connected a practice of self-help against the flaws in human life to a view of the world.

Criticism: betrayal of the past

The humanization of the world, as exemplified by the teachings of Confucius, comes up short by the standard of its fidelity to the aspirations shared by the religious revolutions of the past. Most immediately, it offers too limited a justification for the effort to devalue or to overturn the social divisions within humankind. The chief civilizing device of the humanization of the world is the dialectic between the roles, rules, and rituals of society and the development of our dispositions. Our induction into roles, rules, and rituals teaches us to abandon our primitive self-centeredness. It begins to form in each of us a nature turned to the experience and the aspirations of others. Slowly, this now-socialized nature of ours is elevated and even transfigured by the development of our ability to imagine other people.

The vital question that any such view must face is how will it address the established social regime. A system of roles exhibits a division of labor in society. It forms part of a scheme of social division and hierarchy that includes the class structure of society. Is this scheme to be accepted and rendered more humane, or is it to be defied and reshaped?

In every real historical version of this orientation to existence, the limit of reformist ambition has been to restrain class selfishness and to reshape class in the light of merit. Even the mixture of power, exchange, and allegiance characteristic of the agrarian-bureaucratic societies in which the humanization of the world first arose has been ordinarily accepted as the realistic alternative to endless struggle. There is no vision or energy here to inspire a program of radical reconstruction. Where would such a vision and energy come from if not from a view of the transcending self combined with an idea about our power to change the character as well as the content of the established structures of life and thought?

The abstract idea of society has no natural and necessary translation into any particular way of organizing social life. Are we then to accept the structure that history presents us with in a given society, with all the hierarchies and divisions that it supports and the role of the dead over the living that it embodies? Are the conformity of advantage to merit (as assessed by some collective or governmental authority) and the restraint of power by regard for others to serve as our only reprieves from these forces?

Criticism: betrayal of the future

The humanization of the world offers no usable point of departure for the changes that deserve to be central to any future religious revolution. Two of its limitations render it incapable of serving this purpose. One has to do with its response to the flaws in existence, the other with its inadequacy as an antidote to the risks of belittlement.

One feature of the humanization of the world is its acknowledgment of the facts of mortality and of groundlessness. However, it acknowledges them only to turn decisively away from them to the construction of a human order designed on our scale and according to our concerns. Such is the strategy of the anti-metaphysical metaphysics: finding ourselves in a cosmos that we can understand and master only minimally, facing the certainty of annihilation, and denied insight into the ground of being, we can nevertheless develop, within this inhuman world, a world of our own.

No approach to existence seems more modest or realistic in its attitude to the failings in life. The consequence, however, of this movement of aversion – the turning away from our unmanageable terrors to our feasible tasks – is to deny us some of the means with which to awaken from a half-conscious life of convention, compromise, and routine to a refusal of death by installments. It is not enough, however, to recognize the incurable defects in the human condition only to then contrive to forget them as quickly and as completely as possible. It is necessary to use our confrontation with them as a step in our rise.

In turning away from what is irreparable in our circumstance, the humanization of the world also fails to show the way to remedy what we can repair: our susceptibility to belittlement. As a result, it fails to do justice to the idea that has come to exert a revolutionary influence throughout the world: the notion that every man and woman shares in attributes that we ascribe to God (whether or not such a God exists) and that we can increase our share in those attributes by changing the organization of society and by reorienting the conduct of life.

The ruling ambition of the humanization of the world is to achieve harmony in self and society. It seeks to foster the development of a life in society that gives responsibility to others. Its program is to combine the enhancement of our collective powers with the diminishment of our cruelty to one another. Its prescription for the attainment of this goal is for each of us to do his part in the station that fate and merit have allotted to him even as he cultivates his powers of imaginative empathy.

For these reasons it is unsuited to serve as an instrument of spiritual revolution. At least it will be ill-equipped to serve a spiritual revolution that rejects our belittlement while also acknowledging our mortality, our groundlessness, and our insatiability.

STRUGGLING WITH THE WORLD

Central idea, spoken in sacred and profane voices

A third major option in the spiritual history of humanity has been the struggle with the world. Its central idea is that there is a path of ascent, requiring and enabling us to undergo a transformation of both self and society, which will reward us with an incomparable good, namely, a greater share in the attributes of the divine, or eternal life.

By treading this path, we triumph over evil. (Evil is death and, beyond death, the diminishment of being.) It is our failure to be rescued from what seems to be our condition as hapless and dying organisms unable to discern the reason for our existence and desiring more than we can ever receive. Separation from the divine and from one another presages death and closes the route of escape from this condition. Such separation is itself a beginning of death, because it leaves us blocked and diminished and brings us face to face with our mortality, groundlessness, and insatiability; it bleeds us of our vitality even before we perish.

The struggle with the world has spoken in two voices. One is sacred, that of the Semitic salvation religions – Judaism, Christianity, and Islam – and the other is profane, that of the secular projects of liberation. Both forms convey distinct but analogous messages.

For the sacred form of the struggle with the world, our effort to respond to our mortality, groundlessness, and insatiability is contained within a larger story of transactions between God and humankind. Only because of God's saving work in history can we hope to escape evil and attain a higher, eternal life. History is a significant, but incomplete, scene of salvation rather than an epiphenomenal backdrop to our ascent or to our fall. What begins in history continues beyond history. A change in the character of our relations to one another forms a crucial part of our rescue. Through such a change we confirm our reception of divine grace and lift ourselves above death, groundlessness, and insatiability. The true meaning and potential of our relations to one another become manifest only in the interactions between God and humankind.

For the profane form of the struggle with the world, there is no one here but us. It has manifest in the political programs of liberalism, socialism, and democracy as well as the romantic movement, especially the global popular romantic culture, with its message of the godlike dignity of ordinary men and women and the unfathomable depth and reach of their experience.

Metaphysical vision

The struggle with the world develops against the background of a vision of reality and of our place in it. This vision often remains implicit in ideas about the path of our ascent, through transformation and self-transformation, to triumph over death and to a greater share in the attributes of divinity. But to this day, after centuries of unrivaled influence, this vision has not fully penetrated the consciousness of many of those who claim to be unconditionally loyal to it.

This metaphysical vision is based on a number of presuppositions. Foremost, *there is one real world.*[20] The most important fact about the world is its scandalous particularity: the world is what it is and not something else. The idea of the one real world stands in opposition to the view that our world is one of many worlds existing in parallel or passing from possibility to actuality. Under this latter view, the "one real world" cedes some of its reality to the many other actual ones and appears simply as a precarious and evanescent variation on the workings of nature.

Second, *time is inclusively real.* Time is not an illusion, as the more radical versions of the metaphysic of the overcoming of the world represent it to be, nor, as many of our established ideas about causation and the laws of nature imply, does it touch only certain aspects of reality. It holds sway over everything: nothing is exempt from its influence.

Our conventional beliefs about causality equivocate about the reality of time. They imply that time is real but not too real. If time were not real, causation, as we conventionally understand it, would not exist. Effects must come after causes. Without time, causation can be reduced to logical implication: effects become as simultaneous with their causes as the conclusions of a syllogism are with its premises. If, however, time is inclusively real, and the laws of nature can at least in principle evolve, discontinuously, together with the phenomena that they govern, our causal explanations no longer have immutable warrants. They are adrift on changing laws of nature. Causation would then mean something different from what our conventional beliefs take it to mean or it would be prior to the laws of nature rather than derivative from them. Causality is better regarded as a primitive feature of nature, which may or may not assume recurrent lawlike form.

Third, *the new can happen.* In the vision that is required by the struggle with the world, new – really new – events can take place in the world. The really new is not countenanced by the preexisting structures of reality and by the laws of nature prevailing at the time. It truly violates them and not just our understanding of what they are. It evolves together with them.

The availability of surprise in the world and the human capacity to cause surprise – even to ourselves – are integral to the struggle with the world in all its forms, sacred and profane. The ability to surprise in the sense of acting outside the script of both the social order and the individual character forms part of what vitality means.

Fourth, *history is open.* The openness of history means that its course does not conform to a script. We can reorganize the arrangements of society and culture so that they supply the instruments and multiply the occasions for their own remaking. History thus becomes more open to our transformative action. The result adds substance and luster to our ascent. It makes us freer and bigger. It increases our share in some of the attributes that believers in the salvation religions ascribe to God.

The dominant approaches to the understanding of society and history deny the openness of history to one degree or another. Classical European social theory, as most fully exemplified by the work of Karl Marx, affirmed the idea that the structures of society are human artifacts, which we can reimagine and remake. However, it compromised this revolutionary insight by embracing a series of necessitarian superstitions: that there is a closed list of indivisible institutional systems realized successively in the course of history, that each of these institutional orders amounts to an indivisible system, and that inexorable laws of historical change drive forward the succession of systems. These superstitions of false necessity prevented the thesis of the artifact-like character of social order from ever being carried to its radical and true conclusion. In this manner, the whole order of society is frozen politics, where a temporary containment of struggle reigns over the terms of social life. In these ways, our ruling ideas about society and history prevent us from making sense of the openness of history and deny us guidance about how to make it more open.[21]

Fifth, *the self has unfathomable depth.* We can best approach the meaning of this part of the vision that informs the struggle with the world by considering to what it stands opposed, namely, the reduction of the self to its social station. Such stations place us as protagonists within an established plan of social division and hierarchy. The individual becomes the embodiment of his caste, his community, or his role. He acts out the plan that his station lays in his hands.

Sixth, *the ordinary has more promise than the high-flown.* "I shall pour out my spirit upon all flesh," declares God in the Hebrew Bible. Ordinary men and women have the spark of the divine for the struggle with the world. They are embodied spirit, un-resigned to belittling circumstance. They can ascend, whether or not with the help of divine grace. Their power to rise – to increase their share in the attributes of divinity or to come closer to God or to the god-like within themselves – presupposes and produces a subversion of the hierarchies of the noble and the base in which all the historical civilizations have traded.

The resulting form of moral consciousness teaches us that it is better to look for trouble than to stay out of trouble. It teaches us that our raising up begins in a willed acceptance of heightened vulnerability to disappointment, disillusionment, and defeat; that in throwing down our shields, we regain the first condition of vitality; and that no standard of moral or aesthetic judgment that accepts the hierarchies of the social order deserves anything other than suspicion and resistance.

Criticism: strength and weakness of the struggle with the world

No version, sacred or profane, of the struggle with the world has ever been fully realized in society and culture. To the extent that it has come close to being realized, it has betrayed its central message and has thereby become reduced in doctrine and massively violated in practice. It coexists unresistingly with beliefs, institutions, and practices that contradict its central vision. The result is that in its real historical life, the struggle with the world has existed almost exclusively in such compromised forms. Its visible expressions are the organized varieties of Judaism, Christianity, and Islam as well as conventional secular humanism, with its complacent moral and political pieties.

The message of the struggle with the world survives supine as well as besieged. The ideas and discursive practices that would make it intelligible and usable have never been fully developed. Existing societies, even when they rescue people from the extremes of poverty and oppression, fail to establish a form of life responsive to the promises of this spiritual orientation by failing in their economic, social, and political institutions.

The economic institutions of these societies are organized to deny the mass of ordinary men and women the means with which to live and work as the context-transcending agents that they are. The hereditary transmission of economic and educational advantage through the family continues to reproduce the realities of a class society, inhibiting our power to formulate and enact life-enhancing projects. Wage labor, viewed by the liberals and socialists of the nineteenth century as an inferior form of free labor - and one that bears the taint of serfdom - is now regarded as the natural and even necessary form of free labor. What those liberals and socialists saw as the higher, more perfect expressions of free labor - self-employment and cooperation - remains, or has become, its peripheral form.

Our responsibility to strangers in the societies of the present is largely reduced to money transfers organized by the state through the system of redistributive taxation and social entitlements. Money, however, supplies fragile social cement. It cannot replace direct engagement with others beyond the boundaries of the family and the barriers of family selfishness. The lack of any practical expression of the principle that every able-bodied adult should have some responsibility to care for others outside his own family, as well as a place in the system of production, deprives social solidarity of an adequate basis. The result is to sharpen the contrast between the intimate realm of personal attachment and a heartless world of dealings with strangers.

The political institutions of contemporary societies continue to make change depend upon crisis. They are not designed to increase the temperature of politics or to hasten its pace. Democracy consequently fails to serve as an antidote to the rule of the dead over the living and as a device by which to subordinate structure to will and imagination.

From these successive accommodations result the fossilized forms of Judaism, Christianity, and Islam, preserved as ways to kill time and to deny death. They stand as the evisceration of the ideological programs of the last two centuries; the consequent confinement of would-be leftists and progressives to the work of humanizing a regime that they find themselves unable to reshape; and the pieties of the conventional secular humanism, succeeding the dangerous illusions of romanticism. The real form of this orientation to existence, the character of its presence in history, is the one defined by these many and cumulative surrenders. In this way, its votaries have tried to adapt the message to the world rather than to adapt the world to the message.

Criticism: estrangement from life in the present

The struggle with the world orientation remains the most promising point of departure for our self-understanding, and in order to attempt to change society and ourselves. Nevertheless, in all its contemporary forms, both secular and sacred, it is radically defective. It must be remade or replaced.

Under the aegis of the struggle with the world, our supreme good always lies in the future. This supreme good is defined by that which brings us closer to the divine, to the largest life, to the fullest reality, or to the greatest value; the orientation may situate it in life beyond death or a future social order that restores us to ourselves and empowers us. Either way, the future offered is not the future of our mortal lives, lived in biographical time. Every version of the struggle with the world claims that our orientation to this future good changes immediately our present situation. Our present experience participates, according to such claims, in the future good.

Living for the future in any of the sacred or secular forms advocated by the struggle with the world threatens to estrange us from the present moment and therefore from life itself as it is lived in the succession of present moments rather than as it may be evoked by memory or anticipation. Thus, we squander by our own folly, as if smitten by desire for an absolute that we project forward in time, the most important good, indeed the only good.

The most important objection to the struggle with the world is that it seduces us into war against the matchless good of life lived in the present and gives us in exchange a counterfeit good, the future. The solution to this problem requires a change of vision and of conduct. To bring about such a change is the work of the religion of the future.

COMMON ELEMENTS OF THE ORIENTATIONS

The religions and philosophies that became the bearers of the three orientations to life that I explore here shared something significant in common, notwithstanding the immense differences among them. What could be common among early Buddhism (as an instance of overcoming of the world), early Confucianism (as an example of humanizing the world), and the Near Eastern salvation religions, Judaism, Christianity, and Islam (as the earliest and most powerful expressions of the struggle with the world)? Not only did they represent the place of humans in the world in radically different ways, but they also prescribed starkly different responses to the flaws in our condition. So different were these responses that they may seem to exhaust the major possibilities of ways of contending with the world. Nevertheless, five shared and connected impulses overrode these real differences: a rejection of cosmotheism, anti-nihilism, an emphasis on unity, attack on authority, and ambiguity to state power.

First commonality: rejection of cosmotheism

A first common element of the three major religious orientations is the rejection of cosmotheism, or the identification of the divine with the world. For these orientations, the divine was separated from the world and then placed in relation to it. With this rejection, there began a dialectic of transcendence and immanence that has ever since been central to the religious history of humanity.

There is a basic ambiguity in the rejection of cosmotheism that touches, in its variations, all other aspects of the past religious revolutions. The issue is whether the separation between the world and the divine is merely a shift of view or also a transformative project. Does it suffice to change consciousness, or must we also change the world if we are to establish, in place of cosmotheism, the dialectic of transcendence and immanence?

Second commonality: anti-nihilistic

A second shared attribute of these revolutionary spiritual orientations is their insistence on providing a response to the problem of nihilism aroused by awareness of the flaws in our existence, in particular by our mortality and our groundlessness. By nihilism in this context I mean the suspicion that our lives and the world itself may be meaningless: that they may bear no meaning capable of being translated into the idiom of human concerns. The combination of mortality and groundlessness threatens to reduce existence to hallucination.

In one way or another, these anti-nihilistic messages convey the message that everything is fundamentally all right with the world or will be all right in the end. But for everything to be all right, does it suffice to receive reality in the right way, with a correct understanding and attitude, or must we change the world – and ourselves within it – cumulatively and in a particular direction? Is the struggle with nihilism an argument, such as a metaphysician might have with a skeptic, or is it a campaign of resistance, such as a general might wage against an enemy with vastly superior force?

Third commonality: unity

A third common element is the impulse to affirm the shallowness of the differences within humanity – differences of caste, class, race, nation, gender, role, and culture – by contrast with our fundamental unity. The point is not to deny any measure of reality to these differences or to claim that they are bereft of moral and social consequence but rather to recognize that they pale in comparison to our fundamental unity. The basis of this unity lies not only in our physical constitution but also and chiefly in our predicament, a predicament shaped by our mortality, our groundlessness, our insatiability, and our difficulty in overcoming the disproportion between who we are and how we must live. To be justified, any division within humanity must deepen and develop the unity of humankind. Otherwise, it deserves to arouse suspicion and to be torn down. Until that division is torn down, it should be disregarded in our most important choices and conceptions.

Once again, there is an ambiguity. Is the unity of humankind to be affirmed only as belief or is it to be secured through a reorganization of society? The Stoic could affirm in his heart the fundamental similarity of master and slave without defying the institution of slavery. For him, it might have been enough to show to the other – slave or master – an empathy resulting from the recognition of their fundamental similarity. For the votary, however, the question unavoidably arose as to whether this unity could simply be affirmed as a thesis or needed to be carried out as a program. As a thesis, it would require a change of attitude, a different way of performing within the established roles and arrangements rather than a path to their reshaping. As a program, it might demand the radical reconstruction of the established social arrangements.

Fourth commonality: attack on authority

A fourth shared feature was their attack on the authority and the ascendancy of a prevailing ethic, the ethic of heroic virtue; of power worship; of triumph of the strong over the weak; of winning in every worldly contest; of vindictive reassertion of one's place with regard to others; of glorious recognition, renown, and honor; of manly pride. In each of the civilizations and states within which these religious orientations arose, this heroic and martial ethic was associated with a particular class or caste – the rulers or fighters. The link was especially strong within the structure of the agrarian-bureaucratic empires that formed the most important setting for the emergence of the world-historical religions. What the religious revolutionaries proposed to put in the place of heroic pride and vengeful self-assertion was a sacrificial ethic of self-bestowal, of disinterested love: the agape of the Septuagint, the *ren* of the *Analects*, the world-renouncing self-abandonment of the Buddha. The result was a radical reversal of values: more than a rejection of the ethic of the class/caste of rulers and warriors, it was a turning upside down of it.

There was in this turn, as in all the other shared features, an ambiguity. Was this love to be a fleshless benevolence on the part of the enlightened or the saved? Was it to be handed down from on high and from a distance – with sacrifice but without inner risk – to the unenlightened and the unredeemed? Or was it a love that required from the lover that he unprotect himself and accept a heightened vulnerability? To the extent that it was the former, it might represent, as Nietzsche saw, the continuation of the power impulse in the ethic of valor and vengeance in even more potent and twisted form: the practice of altruism confirming the superiority of the benevolent will without ever placing the agent in intimate jeopardy or acknowledging his need of his self-sacrifice for the supposed beneficiary. If, however, it was the latter, it required from the lover much more than altruism: it required empathetic imagination toward the other person, the unprotection of the self and the recognition of its need for the other, the acceptance of the risk of rebuff or failure.

Fifth commonality: ambiguity to state power

A fifth common characteristic of these religious revolutions lay in their ambiguous relation to the real world of power and of states in history. Each of the orientations to life exemplified by the religions originating from these spiritual upheavals has been a two-sided ticket. One side of the ticket admitted the individual to a triumphal procession - a culture or a collectivity, embraced by a civilization and by a state informed by the orientation's doctrine. By using the ticket, the individual joined the winners, even when the doctrine was one that claimed to exalt the losers. Participation in a community of belief, supported by worldly power and accredited by cultural authority, established a union among the believers that transcended both kinship and social station.

The other side of the ticket authorized the individual to escape from the nightmare of history and the savagery of society into a realm of inner experience in which other standards held. Even the humanization of the world (as in Confucianism), with the central value that it placed on the moral logic of our engagement in society, offered the individual refuge from the verdict of history: an inner life that would be proof against the seductions of worldly power and the demons of worldly failure.

The two-sided ticket of admission and escape is essential to understanding the immense effect exerted by the spiritual approaches arising from these religious revolutions. To understand these religions in the spirit of this two-sided ticket meant, however, to diminish the transformative significance of their teaching. At every point, there was another option: to tear up the two-sided ticket in favor of a progressive attempt to change both self and society and to widen our part in the attributes of divinity. It is at once the most general and the most explicit form of the same ambiguity touching all the other shared characteristics of these spiritual orientations.

CHAPTER 3

Deep Freedom: The Politics of the Religion of the Future

THE TOPIC OF THIS CHAPTER is the meeting of religion and politics. It takes the vantage point of religion rather than the vantage point of politics (the latter being the standpoint from which religion and politics have generally been viewed in the history of Western political thought since Machiavelli and Hobbes). Instead of asking what politics should do with religion, as have most thinkers throughout history, I ask what religion – the religion of the future – should do to politics. Such a political theology begins in a religious conception: the conception of a free society. In this way, the religious revolution for which I argue includes a political revolution.

The argument begins with an outline of the general conception of a free society and what it means. I then enumerate four principles to inform the organization of the free society. These are apostasy, or the means to reject and rebel, plurality, deep freedom, and higher cooperation. The last is the most involved in the politics of the religion of the future and the vision of the free society and bears four key features - equality, cooperation vs. innovation, entrepreneurism and innovation, and imagination - which I outline in the final section.

Conception of a Free Society

A free society is a society whose arrangements express and honor the truth of personality as embodied spirit – a truth upheld in one measure or another by all versions of the struggle with the world and developed more radically by the religion of the future. A simple way to describe the task of developing the conception of a free society is to say that it seeks to go on from where the classical liberals and socialists left off. The aim must be to reject their institutional dogmatism and to revise our hopes for the future in light of the subsequent history of thought and society. In so doing, we teach ourselves to hope for more rather than for less, as we have been persuaded to do by those who have lent the prestige of philosophy to the interruption and containment of the struggle with the world. Such an effort retakes with redoubled force the determination of the liberals and socialists of the nineteenth century to marry the vision of a greater life with the commitment to change the institutional structure of society.

The following outline of the conception of a free society should be read in the context of my subsequent defense of a direction of institutional change.

Consider first the conception of a free society in light of its implications for the relation of the self to the structure of society and then for the relation of the individual to other people. In each of its aspects, the conception describes a limit or an ideal that acquires greater meaning through the demarcation of a pathway of institutional change.

In a free society, the individual has the educational equipment, as well as the economic and political occasion, to cross the frontier between the activities that take the framework for granted and those that bring it into question. The individual has been educated in a way that enables the mind as imagination to become ascendant over the mind as machine. He has learned to philosophize by acting, in the sense that he recognizes in every project the seed of some great or small reformation. The practices of society and of culture multiply opportunities for the affirmation of this preeminence of the mind as imagination over the mind as a formulaic device.

The individual is secure in a haven of protected vital interests and of capability-generating endowments – above all, those of original and continuing education – that enable him fearlessly to face innovation and instability in the social and economic world that he inhabits. His sense of identity and of security is not invested in the permanence of a particular form of collective life. He does not act or think at the behest of a social or cultural script that assigns him a role and tells him how to perform it. He recognizes that the performance of roles gives rise to expectations and obligations, but none so weighty that they automatically trump loyalties to people or devotions to tasks. Roles are to be sometimes used and sometimes bent and stretched, so long as this bending and stretching does not result in betrayal of individuals.

His life chances are not determined by the hereditary transmission of economic and educational advantage through the family. Inequalities of circumstance are outlawed to the extent that they either arise from inequalities of respect and of opportunity or result in them (as universally happens in a class society). Similarly, they are prohibited if they either reflect or reproduce privileged strangleholds on the political, economic, or cultural resources with which we define the future within the present. No free society can have a class structure. An especially poisonous form of such a structure is one that relegates a group of people to a degree of absolute poverty or relative deprivation that not only undermines equality of respect and opportunity but also destroys the practical conditions of self-reliance and self-construction.

In view of the relation between the individual and other people, the conception of a free society requires that the individual not be subject to any form of coercion by others, either directly at the hands of individuals or indirectly at the hands of a state acting as their instrument. (A single-minded focus on oppression by the state, in contrast to many other forms of belittlement, has been a hallmark of many conceptions of a free society.) A free man or woman is not to be coerced materially or spiritually. His or her humanity-defining attribute of transcendence is to be respected and encouraged at every turn.

In a free society, economically dependent wage work is understood (as the liberals and socialists of the nineteenth century saw it) as a temporary and defective compromise. It gives way, increasingly, to self-employment and cooperation, separately or combined, as superior forms of free labor. As soon as the relative wealth and technological and scientific advance of society permit, no person is required to do the repetitious work that is properly consigned to machines. We use machines in such a society to do everything that we have learned how to repeat, so that the whole time of our lives can be reserved for the not yet repeatable.

Cooperation in a free society requires neither sameness nor inclusive agreement. It is energized by difference and disagreement. Differences are less the problem than they are the solution, because they generate the material on which the selective mechanisms of economic competition and organized political rivalry can operate. The differences that we create matter more than the ones we inherit and remember; prophecy counts for more than memory.

The religion of the future turns this attitude into a comprehensive view of our identity and vocation. In so doing, it lends further support to the conception of a free society here outlined. The value of this support is, however, qualified by the ineradicable contestability of any such comprehensive view. A continuing theme of this book is that our commitment to any approach to the problems of existence can enjoy no definitive justification. Our demands always exceed, immeasurably, the grounds for making them. The demand says, "Follow me," but it can never give a conclusive reason to do so. All that it can do is to make an incomplete argument and a defeasible appeal. It cannot escape the circularity in all our large-scale transformative projects: for better or worse, each of them is a partly self-fulfilling prophecy. If it is embraced and if it works, it remakes part of experience in its image. The conception of a free society and the religion of the future from which it may draw energy and authority are no exception to this rule. They are by their very nature endeavors that ask to be judged by the form of life and the type of humanity that they make possible.

FOUR PRINCIPLES: APOSTASY, PLURALITY, FREEDOM, COOPERATION

The task now is to formulate and to justify the principles that should govern the political commitments of the religion of the future and inform the organization of a free society. The task is to understand the practical implications for political life of the overlap between religion and politics, made manifest by the central role in politics as well as in the religion of a conception of human nature that is both descriptive and prescriptive. It is to see how we can establish our freedom rather than our religion, but establish it in a manner that remains faithful to the twofold truth of transcendence and groundlessness. It is to discover how we can best preserve and enhance the openness of political life to the future once we have abandoned the mirage of an institutional order that is neutral among clashing social ideals and among conceptions of humanity.

I address this task by stating and defending four principles. Together, they mark the ground on which a freedom-preserving democracy can be reconciled with the beliefs central to the religion of the future, without reliance on the illusory attempt to establish institutional arrangements neutral among conceptions of the good. These four principles are the principles of apostasy, plurality, deep freedom, and higher cooperation. I take them each in turn.

The principle of apostasy

The first principle of political life viewed from the perspective of the religion of the future is the safeguarding of apostasy. That it is to say, not only the safeguarding of dissent from the religion of the future but also of vehement opposition to it.

The first reason to safeguard the privilege of apostasy is to recognize and honor in the organization of political life the dialectic of transcendence and engagement that helps define our humanity. We cannot become more human by becoming more godlike if we confront a social ideal that we cannot attack. We would have to be able to distinguish institutional arrangements, susceptible to criticism and change, from an idea held above criticism. We can make no such distinction. The law is the institutionalized form of the life of a people, understood and elaborated by reference to the understandings of the ideals and of the interests that make sense of it. If the rejection of the ideal of the neutrality were not to be accompanied by the safeguards to apostasy, those who fear that the failure of neutrality would undermine freedom would be right.

The second reason to ensure the prerogative of apostasy is to guarantee that the regime can be corrected. Only the internal enemies of the established order can guarantee its corrigibility, for it is they and they alone who can subject it to radical opposition. Corrigibility is not a minor attribute of the regime; it is one of its most important features. Its centrality results from awareness of the deficient and ephemeral character of every institutional design. The protection of apostasy is thus closely linked with the integrity of a free society: its continuing power to renew itself, the better to create the new.

It is not enough to protect apostasy negatively. It is also desirable to equip a dissident consciousness with the practical means with which to sustain a form of life and to advocate its virtues, including access to the means of mass communication. Federalism should be stretched to allow different parts of the country or sectors of the society to develop counter-models of the social future. These affirmative instruments must, however, be subject to two vital qualifications.

A first qualification is that the dissident group not be allowed, in the name of its distinctive vision, to oppress its members or to deny them as children the public education that can empower them to rebel against the community or the faith in which they happen to have been born.

A second qualification is that the individual be free to escape to another country, constituted in a different way on the basis of different understandings. Thus, the division of the world into independent states is not only a condition for the development of the powers of humanity; it is also an indispensable safeguard of freedom.

The radical protection of apostasy that these arguments and proposals express may seem too extreme to be compatible with the stability of a political order and with the cohesion of a society. In fact, a regime that cannot withstand such a challenge and prosper in the midst of its unarmed internal enemies is not worth saving. In committing ourselves to the protection of apostasy, we make a double bet. We gamble that dissent and innovation go hand in hand and that innovation is the most important condition of worldly success. We also venture that, once enjoyed, the benefits of a greater freedom, developed for the sake of a greater life, will prove to be irresistible.

The principle of plurality

It is not enough to respect the prerogative of apostasy from the visions of the good and the ideals of humanity informing the regime. Rather, it is also necessary to organize a permanent experiment – both worldwide and in the space of the independent states of the world – regarding the institutional arrangements of a free society. The apostates may dissent from the ideals and the visions associated with the free order, with the sacred or profane versions of the struggle with the world, or with their radicalization and reformation by the religion of the future. The votaries of these projects will and should diverge among themselves in their understanding of the institutional implications of their commitments. Such divergence is not an accidental or passing restraint on the revolutionary ideas to be overcome by convergence and consensus: it is a permanent feature both of the truth about politics and of the truth about freedom.

Consequences follow from the principle of plurality. A first consequence is that the organization of the world should be hospitable to collective experimentation with the alternative forms of a free society. It should not make the arrangements for security or for trade depend upon submission to a particular institutional formula. It should be marked by an institutional minimalism rather than by an institutional maximalism: the greatest economic and cultural engagement of peoples with one another on the basis of the least restraint on their domestic institutional experiments. Arrangements for world trade, for example, should not prevent experiments in the reshaping of a market economy, including those that associate government with private firms or that innovate in the basic rules of property and contract in the effort to organize multiple ways to decentralize economic initiative and organize access to the resources and opportunities of production.

Another consequence of the principle of plurality is that each area of the life of a free society should be organized in a way that empowers experimental divergence in that domain. The capacity to innovate in the institutional forms of a free society must be manifest in the organization of each part of the regime according to the distinctive problems and opportunities of each. Every area of social life should exemplify and enhance the denaturalization of the social regime. For example, market economies remain fastened to a particular version of the idea of a market order, embodied in their systems of private law and often justified as the natural and necessary expression of spontaneous order in economic life. Alternative regimes of property and contract should instead come to coexist experimentally, gaining a greater or lesser foothold in different parts of the economic order. As a result, freedom to recombine factors of production within an unchallenged framework of production and exchange would extend into freedom to innovate continuously in the arrangements comprising such a framework.

Likewise, civil societies remain unorganized or unequally organized under the provisions of contract, corporate, and labor law and, as a result, are denied the chance to share directly in the creation of alternative social futures. Civil society should be organized to better share actively and directly in the development of alternative social futures. It should not do so simply through the work of elected officials and of the political parties. One occasion for such participation is engagement in the provision of public services that equip the context-transcending individual. Another opportunity is the generalization of the principle that every able-bodied adult should have at some time a responsibility to take care of other people outside his own family, thus providing social solidarity with a foundation stronger than money.

Similarly, democracies continue to be established in ways that make change depend on crisis. They give power to the dead over the living by enshrining static institutions and constitutions, thereby allowing an established structure to retain, until the next crisis, its semblance of naturalness, necessity, and authority. For democratic politics, the task is not to solidify certain institutions and guarantee the rule of the majority limited by the rights of political and social minorities, but rather to organize democracy as the collective discovery and creation of the new in social life. Constitutional arrangements should not freeze politics but rather hasten the pace of politics and raise its temperature to enable greater popular engagement in public life. Democracy should exploit the experimentalist potential of federalism to generate counter-models of the social future and establish in the state a power to rescue groups from situations of exclusion or disadvantage that they are unable to overcome by the means of collective action available to them.

Thus, to realize the principle of plurality, it is not enough to ensure that different versions of a free society be established under the aegis of separate, sovereign states and be embodied in the legal orders of those states. It is necessary that each nation have at its disposal the arrangements and the ideas enabling it to reinvent markets, democracies, and civil societies. For it is only by the power and practice of such reinvention that the freedom-destroying weight of established structures can be lightened, the power of the past over the future diminished, and prophecy enabled to speak more loudly than memory.

The principle of deep freedom

In the design of institutions, deep freedom has priority over any form of equality of circumstance. Equality of opportunity is a fragmentary aspect of deep freedom. Freedom and equality may be shallow or deep. They are shallow to the extent that they take the established institutional structure for granted and are understood and implemented within the limits of that structure. They are deep insofar as they advance through the reorganization of that structure.

Deep freedom is therefore freedom grasped and realized through change of our institutions and practices, not just through a one-time change but through a practice that can generate future, ongoing change in the institutional order of society. The idea of deep freedom develops through an interplay between the conception of a free society and the institutional arrangements required to make that conception real.

Those who take the priority of equality over freedom to be the keynote of the progressive cause make an unacknowledged and decisive assumption: they accept the established institutional settlement. If they live in the rich North Atlantic countries, the settlement that they chiefly accept is the social democratic compromise of the mid-twentieth century (with its New Deal counterpart in the United States). If they find themselves in another part of the world, they are nevertheless likely to see that compromise as the horizon and limit of our democratic hopes. What that means is after-the-fact redistribution and regulation rather than any reshaping of either production or politics. By the terms of that bargain, any attempt fundamentally to alter the productive and the political arrangements was abandoned. The state was allowed to gain wide-ranging powers to regulate, to redistribute, and to manage the economy countercyclically.

The conservatives are, according to the same way of thinking, those who want to shift the weight of that historical compromise in the direction of freedom and efficiency. For them, freedom is greater room for maneuver within the terms set by the established forms of the market economy and of constitutional democracy: less regulation and less redistribution so that there may be more space for individual initiative and self-determination free from the tutelage of the state.

Shallow freedom and shallow equality are freedom and equality viewed within the restraints imposed by the prevailing institutional settlement. They are false options. They are based on the unwarranted acceptance of the existing institutional framework, the contingent outcome of that last major institutional reformation. They presuppose the validity of a simple and misleading hydraulic model of ideological debate: more market, less state; more state, less market; or a combination of state and market designed to ensure that the inequalities generated by the market are corrected by the redistributive and regulatory activity of the state.

When we demand more than an attempt to humanize the supposedly inevitable, we turn away from shallow freedom and shallow equality to deep equality and deep freedom. Deep equality is the priority granted to some form of equality of circumstance or outcome, achieved through whatever reshaping of institutions may be required to reach this goal. Equality of respect and equality of opportunity are intrinsic to freedom and to the conception of a free society, not just to the radical conception earlier proposed but also to any conception that remains in close connection with the ideals supported by the profane or sacred versions of the struggle with the world. Shallow and deep equality converge in the primacy that they accord to equality of circumstance. This egalitarian commitment may be formulated outright as a prohibition of extreme inequalities of living standards, income, or wealth. Alternatively, it may be qualified by a willingness to countenance whatever inequalities can be justified by their contribution to the circumstances of the worst off, so long as the fundamental principles of equality of respect and of opportunity remain inviolate.

Deep equality is distinguished from shallow equality by its refusal to take the established institutional arrangements for granted, including those that shape the market economy. Its characteristic device is not, as with shallow equality, compensatory redistribution by tax and transfer. It is a change in the institutional arrangements, especially those that organize production and exchange, the better to influence the primary distribution of wealth and income. For example, deep equality is what the Spartans had among themselves, although not with the Helots. It is what Proudhon, William Morris, and many other socialists of the past have desired. It can be secured only by imposing radical restraints on the sale of property and the accumulation of capital.

Who wants deep equality? Not the hundreds of millions who have fled from countryside to city, even when no work awaits them in the city. Not the multitudes who sit transfixed before their screens watching the fantastical narratives of empowerment and escape of popular romantic culture. Not searchers after more consumption, more excitement, more diversion, or more capability. No one wants it who could have, with a measure of abundance, anything else. And when they want it, if indeed they understand it, they want it only as a consolation in the absence of such more appealing goods. Austerity, drudgery, and monotony, a narrowing of alternatives of action, can seem an acceptable form of existence only if they appear to be the sole alternative to stark oppression. Ancient Sparta has few takers.

Deep freedom is the sole defensible political goal of progressives – of those who have understood the political implications of the struggle with the world and who want to rescue this orientation to existence from the compromises and surrenders that continue to circumscribe its reach. It is therefore a political principle of those who move in the direction of the religion of the future. Deep freedom, in its fullest sense, is the dialectic between the conception of a free society and the cumulative institutional innovations that can make this conception real.

There is no stock set of institutional arrangements that, once enacted, make the conception of a free society live in social reality. There is an open array of institutional enhancements, many of them rough and flawed functional equivalents to other such arrangements. What matters is the direction, defined precisely through the interaction between the understanding and its institutional expressions.

The distinction between Right and Left has not lost its meaning. It nevertheless needs to be redrawn. To confine it within the limits of the contrast between shallow equality and shallow freedom is to reduce it to a contrast between two versions of counterrevolutionary thought, both of them antagonistic to the driving political aspirations of the struggle with the world, to be upheld and advanced by the religion of the future.

On this account, the conservatives are those who despair of our power to raise ourselves up through the transformation of our arrangements to a greater life. The progressives are those who insist on transforming the institutional structure of society to the end of achieving a greater life for all. They do not want merely to substitute one structure for another. They want to change the sense in which the structure is a structure by making the social order hospitable to structure-defying structure, which is to say by rendering it friendly to freedom. This transformation may be gradual and piecemeal in its method but nevertheless radical in its outcome if it persists, informed by a developing idea of freedom, in a particular direction.

The practical significance of deep freedom is made clear by spelling out its implications for inequality of circumstance:

1. No inequality of circumstance should be tolerated that threatens either equality of respect or equality of opportunity.
2. Inequalities of circumstance resulting in inequalities of opportunity become especially damaging when they are expressed as privileged holds on the economic, political, or cultural resources. If, for example, the result of an inequality of circumstance is to allow a certain class of society to exert decisive influence over the government under the disguise of democratic institutions and in effect to buy political influence, the system of freedom is violated.

3. Inequalities of circumstance are suspect that have as their consequence the promotion of free labor over the superior forms of self-employment and cooperation.
4. Inequalities of circumstance that result from the reproduction of class society by the hereditary transmission of unequal economic and educational advantage through the family are to be combated.
5. Inequalities of circumstance may be defended by their supposed contribution to the development of the wealth and practical powers of society. However, the inequalities thus justified must never be allowed to accumulate to the point of trespassing on the concerns expressed by the first two ideas (the primacy of equality of respect and of opportunity and the exclusion of inequalities that result in privileged strangleholds on the making of the future). They must be prevented from relegating the mass of ordinary men and women to dependent wage labor or to formulaic, machine-like work (the third idea).
6. We should approach the reconciliation of the fifth idea with the other four in the spirit of an open-minded, experimental, and hopeful search for arrangements lying in the zone of potential intersection between the institutional conditions for the development of the productive capabilities of society and the institutional requirements for the overcoming of domination and dependence in society.

The ideal of equality is best defended when it is subordinated to the greater and more inclusive ideal of deep freedom. For it is this ideal that most directly touches our interest in making ourselves more human by making ourselves more godlike. The revolutionary reach of this ideal becomes clear as soon as we insist on equipping it with its most useful instrument: the institutional reorganization of society.

The principle of higher cooperation

The priority of deep freedom over equality of circumstance necessitates a change in the character of our cooperative practices. This is to say, an idea of cooperation forms part of the conception of a free society. Other things being equal, the more we are able to organize our activities through a division of labor untainted by subjugation and dependence, the freer we become. Insofar as we achieve this goal, we can do more and we can become more, both individually and collectively.

While institutions and education can promote the development of our cooperative capacities, so can a core idea of the past wave of religious revolutions. This idea is an idea of the shallowness of the divisions within humankind. The force of this idea can lead to the denial of class and support the disposition to cooperate across class lines. In moving from the devaluation of social divisions to rejection of the fate of belittlement, the religion of the future establishes the disposition to cooperate with strangers on the strongest foundation that it can have: the basis of our understanding of who we are and of what we can become. No definitive institutional formula can capture the potential for cooperation because none can do justice to our powers of experience and of creation. However, one institutional settlement may be better than another because it enables us to innovate in our cooperative practices.

It may seem strange to consider the content of such a regime in a book on religion that is also a religious book. The religion of the future, however, must resemble the religions of the past two and a half millennia in its impulse to inform the whole of our experience. Moreover, it cannot remain faithful to the image of the person as embodied spirit, which it inherits from the struggle with the world, if it abandons our material life in society to practices and beliefs that weaken and deny our power to resist and revise the context.

FOUR FEATURES OF THE COOPERATIVE REGIME

To move in the direction of deep freedom, a cooperative regime must exhibit four features: equality, cooperation vs. innovation, entrepreneurism and innovation, and imagination. Each of these features needs to be manifest in the institutions defining the regime as well as in the practices and the beliefs reproducing it. These features modify both the organization and the experience of the division of labor in society.

First feature: equality

A first feature of higher cooperation is that each should partake on an equal and open basis. It is necessary that the cooperative regime and the nature and scope of the tasks that each participant undertakes should not be predetermined by any ready-made script resulting from the structure of division and hierarchy in society or from the translation of that structure into a system of stereotyped social roles.

Whether they are members of this or that social class or of this or that community of sentiment or of belief, their respective membership in any of the divisions of humanity should count as little as possible when they meet to cooperate. They should meet not as Robinson Crusoe met a subordinate Friday but as he might have met an alter ego of himself.

Second feature: cooperation vs. innovation

A second trait of a cooperative regime is that it is arranged and understood to moderate the tension between cooperation and innovation – the best regime of cooperation is the one that is most favorable to collective learning and permanent innovation.

It is not enough to cooperate; it is also necessary to innovate. Like the facility for cooperation, the facility for innovation has both a moral and a material aspect. The ability to innovate in organization and ideas as well as in technologies soon overrides the size of the economic surplus over current consumption as the main constraint on economic growth. It is an imperative central to every realm of practical activity, from administration to warfare. It is as well a call to combine people, resources, and machines in ways that step over the limits imposed by established assumptions and arrangements. It uses the transformation of nature as an incitement to the self-transformation of humanity. Innovation requires cooperation. Every step in a process of innovation requires cooperative activity, both to develop the innovation and to implement it. However, every innovation also jeopardizes cooperation, because it threatens to disturb the vested rights and the settled expectations to which an established cooperative regime gives rise.

The single most important condition for success in the effort to reconcile these two imperatives is that the security of the individual in a haven of protected vital interests and endowments be combined with the enhanced plasticity of the surrounding social and economic space. It is a dialectical movement: something is protected, the better to open up a great deal else to experiment and change.

Secure in his protection and empowered by his endowments, the individual is able to confront instability and to thrive in its midst. Such a project reveals the salvageable practical content of the idea of fundamental rights, once we expunge from it its metaphysical and theological veneer. An experiment designed to reconcile flexibility and security in the organization of work represents no more than a fragmentary foreshadowing of this larger vision.

Third feature: entrepreneurism and innovation

A third attribute of a cooperative regime is that it combines a multitude of stimulations to novelty with a remorseless mechanism for the competitive selection of the results. The production of goods and services is the domain of social life most readily exemplifying the practical implications of this principle. The state should encourage a fervor of entrepreneurial activity and innovation. It should also, however, work to ensure that the results of this fervor are subject to draconian competitive selection in the market. The more the state is engaged in encouraging productive activity, the greater the reason to sharpen the subsequent competitive selection.

Consider the example of industrial policy, understood as a term denoting any form of coordinated action between governments and private firms in any sector of the economy. Production normally develops by analogical extension: new lines emerge from established lines. When the circumstance is one of relative backwardness – of a sector of production or of the entire national economy – or the new line runs well in advance of existing lines, the chain of analogies may be thin. Government can then compensate by facilitating access to the missing inputs of credit, technology, capabilities, and staff.

Pluralistic strategic coordination and cooperative competition prefigure innovations in the institutional arrangements of the market economy – innovations designed to make more innovation possible. The integrity and the efficacy of such a scheme of prospective incitement require that it be followed by a radicalization of competitive selection. The institutional innovations that serve the arousal before the fact then become part of the institutional setting of market competition after the fact. It is a connection reenacting in material life the experience of innovation in thought.

From such innovations in the arrangements governing the relation between governments and firms, alternative regimes of contract and property can arise. Each such regime organizes decentralized access to the resources of production and to the opportunities of economic initiative in a different way. Each strikes in different form the balance between giving voice to multiple stakeholders in particular productive resources and ensuring the power of entrepreneurs to bet their stake against dominant opinion. Variation will increase within national economies as well as among them. More people will then be more likely to have more access to more markets, capabilities, and capital in more ways. Diversity, in organization as well as in experience and perspective, will serve as an incitement to fecundity. Because scale will be achieved, for the same reasons and in the same manner, in many different ways rather than only in ways that place the power to direct capital in a small number of hands, competition can more easily be sharpened without imperiling scale. What the fervor creates, the competition will judge.

A similar combination between prospective provocations to invent and retrospective procedures to select can and should be established in the organization of democratic politics as well as in the organization of civil society. The political and social forms of such a combination are, however, less obvious and more subtle than its economic ones. The constitutional arrangements of a high-energy democracy must favor the creation of a broad range of experiments; for example, by allowing particular places and sectors to create counter-models of the national future (the radicalization of the experimental uses of federalism). Yet the power of governments and electorates to overcome impasse and to choose a way forward in the light of such experiments can be enhanced by other arrangements that prevent or overcome impasse between the political branches of governments and engage the people in a continuing conversation about the alternative futures of their country.

A power for decisive action is what we should desire. It should be informed by a vast range of experimental variation within government, the economy, and civil society but subject at every turn to challenges that can result in a change of direction. The dialectic between the experiments in a place or in a sector and the societywide struggle over a direction, subject to reversal, serves as the counterpart in national politics to the sequence of prospective stimulus and retrospective selection in economic life. To act on this analogy is to make both production and politics more closely resemble thought.

Fourth feature: imagination

A fourth feature of higher cooperation follows from the need to narrow the distance between the characteristics of experimental thought and the traits of our political and productive practices. A cooperative regime should take as its regulative ideal to become an embodiment of the imagination in the workings of the division of labor. By recasting our cooperative practices on the model of imagination, we serve many of our most fundamental interests. We establish a setting favorable to innovation in every domain of experience. We oppose the force and influence of any entrenched scheme of social division and hierarchy, given that the power of any such scheme is the enemy of the imagination in social life. We change our relation to established structures by acquiring the power to rethink and remake them in the midst of our ordinary activities. As a result, we improve our chances of advancing in the zone of intersection between the institutional requirements of our material and our moral interests.

The attempt to reshape a cooperative regime on the model of the imagination may seem to provide only the most general and remote guidance in our efforts at institutional reconstruction. Yet it has a wealth of implications for the ordering of practical social life. To understand these implications, consider what such an attempt must reject in the organization of economic and political life:

It must oppose any way of organizing a market economy that fastens the market to a single dogmatic version of itself.

For the same reason, it must rebel against any form of political life that, by lowering the temperature of politics and by slowing down its pace (particularly through the designed perpetuation of deadlock between the political branches of government), inhibits the political transformation of society. The low-energy democracies of today cannot serve as political embodiments of the imagination. One of the marks of the imagination is to do the work of crisis without crisis.

It must not accept a world political and economic order that is hostile to experiments and heresies. Such an order amounts to a conspiracy of the great powers against the place of imagination in the world. The success of this conspiracy depends on lack of imagination as much as it depends on interest and fear.

It must not allow the forces that can most threaten this structure – the visionary and prophetic forces that lie dormant in religion and in high and popular culture – to be privatized and cut off from the public conversation of the democracy.

It must insist that no man or woman be forced to do the repetitious work that can be undertaken by a machine. Our liberation from machine-like jobs depends on the massive economic and cultural changes that would allow us to create non-formulaic jobs in large number. These changes are unlikely in turn to advance far until wage labor begins to give way to some combination of self-employment and cooperation as the predominant form of free labor. The broad mass of ordinary men and women can then become masters of themselves.

In the spirit of envisaging such steps, consider the affinity between our cooperative practices and our imaginative life from the vantage of momentous changes already taking place in the organization of work and production. A new way of cooperating begins to emerge throughout much of the world. Although it has been studied at greatest length as a form of industrial production, it applies as well to other sectors of the economy and to extra-economic activities, from administration to education. Its hallmarks are the weakening of any rigid contrast between conception and execution, the permanent reinvention of specialized work roles, the mixture of cooperation and competition in the same domains, the ongoing revision of the way identities and interests are understood, and the turning of practical activity, whether within or outside of production, into a practice of collective learning and collective innovation.

Will the sectors of practical activity marked by these characteristics remain a worldwide archipelago of islands of experimentalism, from which the vast majority of men and women remain excluded in richer countries as well as in poorer ones? Or will these advanced practices increasingly penetrate and transform wide areas of the society and the economy? The answer to these vital questions depends on the institutional reorganization of market economies, representative democracies, and independent civil societies. Such reorganization cannot take place within the limits of the established institutional and ideological settlement.

DEEP FREEDOM

The emergence of this new way of doing things is not a horse that we can ride to deep freedom. We can nevertheless use it to our larger ends, but only if we redirect and reshape it. Radicalized in method, broadened in scope, and made more inclusive in its social base, it can be made to serve the dissolution of rigid structure and the triumph of imagination over fate.

In the religion of the future's political theology without God, transcendence no longer takes the form of projecting the good – our rise to a greater life or to life eternal – onto a historical or providential future that leaves us estranged from life in the present. Transcendence takes the form of a rejection of the path of least resistance in the circumstance of our time: working with the instruments of the circumstance against the logic of the circumstance and, through such engagement and resistance, beginning right now to make ourselves into what we hope to become.

CHAPTER 4

Becoming Human by Becoming More Godlike: The Conduct of Life in the Religion of the Future

EVERY RELIGION grounds an orientation to existence in a comprehensive view of who we are, what we can become, and our place in the world. The meaning of any such inclusive account becomes clear only through its implications for how to live. It is above all a judgment of its bearing on the conduct of life that we read the message of a religion. It can be no different for a religion of the future.

The earlier argument about the occasions and aims of religious revolution has as its central thesis the claim that the higher religions provide an inadequate basis for our decisions now about how to live and what to do with our lives. It was argued that a reorientation of existence against the background of a reconstruction of society is the prophetic core of a change in our religious beliefs. The task now is first to describe the central idea of such a reorientation for today and, second, to achieve clarity about the form that arguments and proposals about the conduct of life in the religion of the future should take.

The argument is made in three parts. The first part discusses what it means to share in the attributes of the divine and become god-like rather than aspire to be gods. To do this, I argue, we must overthrow the self in a movement from self-subversion to self-transformation. The second part of the chapter then outlines a program for how to live, proposing three virtues to live by - virtues of connection, purification, and divinization – and four characteristics for the course of life – decentering, downfall, mutilation, and mumification. The third and final section explores six antidotes to the acute problem of mummification, or repetition and hardening of the self.

THE ENHANCEMENT OF LIFE AND OVERTHROW OF THE SELF

The change of life that we should seek in light of the earlier arguments of this book is to live in such a way that we die only once. It is also to increase our share in some of the attributes that we ascribe to the divine while renouncing any effort to share in certain other attributes. The widening of our part in the marks of divinity must begin in the recognition of the incalculable distance to be traversed in the course of its pursuit. We squander the good of life by surrendering to a diminished way of being in the world. We settle for routine and compromise. We stagger half-conscious through the world. Anxious for the future, we lose life in the only time that we have, the present. This squandering is a dying many times. Our interest is to stop this dying so that we can live until we die only once.

Viewed from another angle, the purpose of our self-transformation is to increase our share in some of the attributes that we ascribe to the divine while eschewing any effort to possess or to mimic other such attributes. We can make ourselves more god-like in the sense of the first set of attributes. However, we cannot become God: the second set of attributes is not only forever beyond our reach but also incompatible with our humanity.

The qualities to which we cannot and should not aspire are those of eternity, omniscience, and completeness. We cannot aspire to eternity because we are mortal. We cannot aspire to omniscience because we are groundless. We cannot aspire to completeness because we are insatiable. All of our activities take place in a finite world in which we enjoy limited capabilities. The strengthening of our powers can never approach the limit of omnipotence. The essence of Prometheanism, as a sequel to the struggle with the world, is the attempt to become more godlike in precisely this sense, the sense of the attributes that are prohibited to us. The triumphalism, the resentment, and the cruelty accompanying Prometheanism rank among the psychological consequences of this misunderstanding of our condition.

Our share of the divine lies in another direction, the direction of embodied spirit. We transcend finite circumstance. We are also incomplete: it is only by connection with others that we enhance the sentiment of being and developing a self. That all such connections also threaten us with loss of individual distinction and freedom is the contradiction inscribed in our being. This contradiction is most completely resolved, to the extent that it can be resolved at all, in love freely given and freely rebuffed. It is also resolved, although less fully, by the higher forms of cooperation.

The powers to transcend structure and to respond to our incompleteness through love and cooperation are complementary, not contradictory, features of our experience. To the extent that we experience ourselves and act as puppets of an established regime of life, thought, or character, we cannot fully engage other people or the world. In the salvation religions, even the transcendent God is represented as being incomplete: he needs man, whom he creates – a notion disconcerting to the theologians and philosophers who struggled to represent the one and transcendent God in the categories of Greek philosophy.

By transcending structure and living out the implications of our incompleteness through love and cooperation we open ourselves both to other people and to the world. This and this only is the experience of the divine in which we can hope to share, not the inhuman powers that the Promethean wants to claim for humankind. It is with regard that we can aspire to become more godlike by the same means and in the same fashion in which we become more human. The enhancement of life and the sharing of some (but not other) of the qualities that we ascribe to God represent two convergent descriptions of the goal to which our self-transformation is best directed.

A way of living that keeps faith with these concerns, experiences, and ideas must begin in the overthrow of ourselves. By the unwavering recognition of death, groundlessness, and insatiability, we awake to life. In our advance to a greater life, we confront an initial obstacle: we spend our time in a daze of diminished existence, neither awake nor asleep. We resign ourselves to compromise and routine, seeing the world through the categories of the prevailing culture or the methods of established ways of thinking. We reconcile ourselves to the mutilation of our experience that we began to accept when we entered on a particular course of life. We allow ourselves to be subdued by the carapace of diminished experience that formed around us as we grew older. For the vast majority of men and women, economic necessity and drudgery overwhelm and disguise a stupefaction that would otherwise be apparent. For the increasing number of people who, with the material progress of society, are released from grinding material constraint, there is no such disguise. In this way, we cease to live as embodied spirit, as the context-bound but context-resisting agents that we really are. That which is most precious – life itself – we give away in return for nothing. We belittle ourselves, wrongly mistaking our belittlement for a fate as inescapable as our mortality, our groundlessness, and our insatiability.

The antidote to this diminishment is to face the terrifying truth about our situation. Our confrontation with the three great terrors of human life shakes and arouses us, if only we could bring ourselves to reenact it always and to the end. Aroused from our daze, we begin to recover the highest good: life now. We then confront the quandary that we have been taught to appreciate by the achievements and insights of the struggle with the world, as well as by the failures and illusions. We must find a way to live for the future without being estranged from life in the present.

Living for the future means living as beings whose consciousness and trajectory are not finally determined by the present circumstances of their existence. In particular, they are not restricted by the established structure of society and of thought. Such beings are able to envision a greater life and to project the path by which they will reach it. All their deeds and thoughts are premised on insight into the disproportion between who they are, as context-shaped but also context-transcending agents, and the situation in which they find themselves. As a result, they do not regard their susceptibility to belittlement as a flaw to be accepted together with their mortality, groundlessness, and insatiability. They understand the decisive importance of drawing in the right place the line between the immutable circumstances of human life and the alterable organization of society.

THE VIRTUES: CONNECTION, PURIFICATION, DIVINIZATION

Ideas and stories are not enough to ensure that we will awake from the daze of a diminished existence to possess life in the full. To achieve this goal, we must supplement them either by practices that society and culture establish or by virtues that make up for their absence. In the previous chapter, I outlined the core principles of the institutional arrangements and practices required. Below, I turn to the personal virtues. The need of the virtues is directly in response to the following problem: what if the institutional arrangements, as well as the practices that rely on them and that reproduce them, are missing? Then certain habitual dispositions to action – the virtues – must do the work that would otherwise be done by practices and institutions. Political institutions make political virtues not unnecessary but less necessary. We establish political institutions so that we can depend less on these virtues.

Virtues of connection

The threshold obstacle that we face in the making of a self is our self-centeredness. Having discovered in early childhood that the world is not organized around him, the individual resists renouncing his self-centeredness and submitting to the discipline of society. From the perspective of the morality honored in every social and cultural regime, the premise of what we owe one another is that each of us is simply one among many. Even the most hierarchical order insists on engaging those who occupy the highest rank in its hierarchy in a web of reciprocal obligations.

For these reasons, we should not understand the virtues of connection, as the Greeks and Romans did and as the moral philosophers continue to do, as simple restraints upon selfishness – the habits of a reflective altruist. We should understand them in the light of the complications that are inseparable from their place and potential in moral experience. To this end, we must borrow the words of pagan moral philosophy but stretch and bend their meaning.

The first of the virtues of connection is respect. Respect is best understood as the recognition of our common humanity, our sharing in the condition of embodied spirit. The development of such an experience, as many of the religions of the past – Confucianism first among them – have understood, represents one of the highest tasks of civilization. The most important practical expression of respect is an ability to see and to treat another person as more than what he appears to be; that is to say, as more than the occupant of a particular station in society and even as more than the character that he displays in his actions. Respect is a variety of reverence, a worship of that in us which entitles us to renounce our self-hatred for not being God while encouraging us in our hope of becoming more godlike. Such an attitude dismisses the high-handed and self-defensive benevolence concealing the unacknowledged and resentful impulse behind the philosophy of altruism.

A second virtue of connection is forbearance, the restraint that we impose on the expression of our views and on the vindication of our interests so that others may have the space in which to express and to develop theirs. To practice the virtue of forbearance, we must master our ambivalence to others as well as our self-centeredness. Forbearance requires the marriage of self-denial with imagination, or insight into the inner world of other people. A generosity bereft of such insight is in fact a form of cruelty and subjugation incompatible with our respect for one another as context-resistant originals.

A third virtue of connection is fairness, which we should not understand as giving each person his due. We should rather understand treating others fairly as treating them in ways that diminish the price in subjugation with which every connection threatens us and thereby collaborating in self-construction. Fairness, practiced in this way, is a kind of compassion closely linked to respect and forbearance. What our actions say to another person when we treat him fairly is "I will not make you denature yourself in any degree nor will I expect you to serve my will." As a result, you will be a little freer – a little more assured in the sentiment of being – than you were before.

A fourth virtue of connection is courage, the disposition to overcome fear, especially the fear of the harms that we must face to become freer and greater. We become freer and greater by standing up to the structures of society, of thought, and of character, and by refusing, in our relations to others, to settle for the middle distance. This virtue of courage has a decisive bearing on our connections to other people. We cannot become bigger without being courageous. We cannot transform our ties to others in the direction sought by the religion of the future without becoming bigger. Cowardice is belittlement. The acceptance of belittlement negates a defining goal of the spiritual transformation for which the religion of the future speaks and corrupts all of our relations to one another.

With regard to our attachments, the most important form of courage is the acceptance of a greater vulnerability, as indispensable to love as it is unnecessary to altruism. Love cannot be sustained without a lowering of the defensiveness through which we habitually confirm our ambivalence to others. To recognize and receive love requires no less an acceptance of vulnerability than to offer love: in offering it, we risk rebuff and failure; in receiving it, we denude ourselves of part of the paraphernalia of society and stand naked under the gaze of the other. A less radical form of vulnerability is also required by the higher forms of cooperation and by the varieties of community that are built on difference and reciprocal engagement rather than on sameness and mimicry.

With respect to our resistance to circumstance and context, courage begins in our willingness to defy the script that we are handed by the established order of society or of thought and to risk disillusionment as well as isolation. Our ascent is incompatible with the security afforded by a posture of ironic distance from any demanding moral or political faith. To the self-protection of irony, the courage required by the religion of the future prefers the painful dialectic of faith and disillusionment. This dialectic makes possible both self-discovery and discovery of the world. It dissolves the routines and compromises that rob us, little by little, of life.

Virtues of purification

The virtues of purification address belittlement. They work to help distinguish the central from the peripheral in existence and our consequent absorption in concerns that separate us from ourselves and divert us from the enhancement of life. This absorption in the peripheral amounts to an aspect of the diminished experience of life that it must be the purpose of our self-overthrow to overcome.

A first virtue of purification is simplicity. Simplicity is the disposition to renounce the material and immaterial bric-a-brac of ordinary experience for the sake of focus on what matters: our devotion to others and our wrestling with the institutional, conceptual, and character-ontological settings of our existence. The commitment of consciousness to the trivial amounts to a lesser idolatry. It squanders our ultimate resource – time – in efforts bearing no relation to either of the two chief aspects of our experience: reconciliation with other people and overthrow of the dictatorship of context – whether of society, thought, or character – in which we move. By practicing the virtue of simplicity, we signify our intention to recognize the value of every moment and prepare ourselves to overcome estrangement from life in the present.

A second virtue of purification is enthusiasm. Enthusiasm is readiness to give oneself to an activity that, once it is found not to disregard the virtues or to violate the obligations of connection, absorbs us for a while without residue or reservation and seems to be eternal while it lasts. In the experience of enthusiasm we have a partial antidote to the sufferings of mortality, groundlessness, and insatiability. It is one that does not depend on self-deception or require indifference.

A third virtue of purification is attentiveness. Attentiveness completes the work of simplicity and enthusiasm. It is their consummation and reward. Through the virtue of attentiveness, we turn to the manifest world and approach the ideal of a mind on which nothing is lost. The perceptual immediacy of the world in childhood, celebrated by the poet as a lost paradise, is recaptured by the grown man as intensified and discriminating vision. An aspect of the recovery of this immediacy is our capacity to recover the sense of the strangeness of what appears to be natural as well as of the excess of nature over established thought.

If simplicity and enthusiasm serve chiefly as instruments by which we cease to be in thrall to context, attentiveness describes principally our relation to the reality beyond the self and its contexts of society, thought, and character. Our relative openness to the promptings of the manifest world is a mark of embodied spirit and a sign of the enhancement of life in a human being. If genius, rather than thinking better, sees more, then attentiveness enables the attentive to share in the experience of genius.

Virtues of divinization

The problems to which the virtues of divinization respond are those that the religion of the future takes as its first inspiration, namely, the correction of our belittlement, the overcoming of the gap between our self-understanding as embodied spirit and the ordinary circumstances of existence, and the striving to extend our share in the attributes of the divine.

The first virtue of divinization is to accept risk and vulnerability by moving toward life rather than away from it: more engagement, more connection, more commitment, more risk, more vulnerability. It is to prefer the life-giving dialectic of faith, disillusionment, and revised faith to the life-narrowing posture of ironic distance and self-protection. The result manifests itself in the cultivation of a hopeful and patient availability, availability to this dialectic and to the suffering that it exacts.

The two other virtues are openness to the other person and openness to the new. Openness to the other is what the doctrine of the relation of self to others teaches. The religion of the future takes this view over from the struggle with the world and pursues it free of the equivocations that surround it in that tradition. Its supreme form is personal love among equals rather than benevolence offered from on high or from a distance. Its more diffuse expressions, outside the circle of our closest attachments, are communities cemented by difference rather than by sameness and the higher forms of cooperation organized institutionally in the practices of production, politics, and civil society. Its work is the same as its presupposition: attenuation of the conflict between our need for other people and our need to escape the jeopardy in which they place us.

Openness to the new is the virtue that describes the moral consequence of the doctrine of the relation of spirit to structure. The religion of the future inherits this doctrine from the struggle with the world and radicalizes it. This virtue acts out the human truth of our relation to the settled contexts of our life and thought. That these contexts are ephemeral and defective, that they cannot accommodate all the experience and insight we have reason to value, that there is always more in us individually and collectively than is or ever can be in them are facts giving us persistent reason to rebel against structures. In rebelling against them, we must seek to change their character as well as their content, their relation to our structure-defying freedom. If we surrender to them and allow them to have the last word rather than keeping the last word for ourselves, we interrupt our attempt to increase our share in the attributes of divinity. We cease to be fully human.

The practice of the virtues of divinization modifies the meaning and content of the virtues of connection. It turns respect into compassion or fellow feeling, forbearance into self-sacrifice, and fairness into mercy. It also changes the experience – central to the virtues of purification – of losing the self the better to regain it. The ascent of the self, through simplicity, attentiveness, and enthusiasm, now undergoes a decisive reorientation. Instead of keeping out of trouble to achieve composure, the self looks for trouble to find, affirm, and express its own infinity.

THE COURSE OF LIFE: DECENTERING, DOWNFALL, MUTILATION, MUMMIFICATION

I have just presented the moral agenda of the religion of the future as a doctrine of the virtues. In a convergent and complementary statement, I now restate the moral agenda as a conception of our response to certain universal points of inflection in human existence. It will be surveyed through four stages: decentering, downfall, mutilation, and mummification.

Decentering

Early in childhood, every human being finds out that he is a distinct self and that this self is not the center of the world. He discovers that there are other human beings and that he is one among many. This discovery occurs so early that it seems to be coeval with the birth of consciousness in the experience of a boundary between each of us and other people. Having found that we are only one among many and that the consciousness of another person is not only distinct from ours but also all but inaccessible to us, we long for acceptance and recognition of our worth and our very existence in the world. This unlimited longing for others is riven by an ambivalence, however. From this ambivalence we win release only when we settle, uneasily, into the middle distance of indifference. In that middle distance, however, we can never win the prize of the unconditional assurance that we seek.

The only axis of our moral development that can offer the prospect of attenuating our ambivalence is one that moves from love to community. In this movement, the conflict between the enabling conditions of self-assertion is moderated, going from love (in our most intimate experience) to a community based upon reciprocal engagement and recognized difference rather than similarity or sameness (in our continuing attachments). From there, it extends to the reform of the division of labor in the spirit of the higher forms of cooperation.

Downfall

A second formative incident in the course of life is our evasive encounter with death and groundlessness. It takes place not long after our decentering and results in a second and more decisive downfall. Instead of seeking vainly to reverse it, we find that our interest is to recognize in it one of the conditions of a higher existence.

We can respond in ways that help us enter into the possession of life. One such response is engagement in activities that command all of our passion. In those activities, the hold of each of the irreparable defects of life on our experience of life is temporarily suspended. Insatiable desire comes to rest: it finds an object and an expression that seem adequate to our context-transcending humanity. In such engagement, we respond to our groundlessness by means of activities that command our attention and generate their own terms of reference and of justification. If ever there were truth in the idea of creating meaning in a meaningless world, it would be in such a circumstance.

In this situation of total abandon to all-consuming activity, we are released for a while from the bonds of time. It is the closest acquaintance we can ever hope to have with the timeless. At the limit, it abolishes both the selective memory of the past and the anticipation or apprehension of the future and places us in an eternal present, from which our time-obsessed conscious life drives us out.

The repair of the incurable defects of human existence by these occasional experiences of self-abandonment to what elicits passion is not for keeps, however. We do not in fact abolish by virtue of such experiences our mortality, our groundlessness, or our insatiability. The sense of overcoming that may attend these activities is in fact a hallucination. Life waits outside; once the passion is spent and the spell is broken, it fills the prose of reality. It is only on the condition of acknowledging and accepting our mortality and our groundlessness that we can possess it undiminished.

Mutilation

The marks of life – surfeit, fecundity, and spontaneity – reveal the indefinite range of experience and initiative of which, barring great misfortune, every individual human being is capable. Part of the condition of embodied spirit is to enjoy such acquaintance with many ways of being and many forms of consciousness.

Each of us must then determine how he is to live in society in such a way that his existence does not come to represent a denial and subversion of his nature as context-transcending spirit. In this pursuit, he faces a third decisive incident in the normal course of existence. He cannot be anything or everything, anyone or everyone; rather, he must become someone in particular. To become someone in particular, he must renounce many other forms of humanity that might become his.

This imperative of ceasing to be many things in order to become one thing – of abandoning many possibilities of existence the better to develop one – is a mutilation. We face this mutilation in two major variations: the need to develop a course of life and the requirement to occupy a station in society. A course of life and a station in society are so closely linked that it may be hard to distinguish between them. Nevertheless, they present us with the problem of mutilation in different registers. The course of life has to do with the trajectory of an existence, beginning in the dreams of youth and ending in death, and with the relation of that trajectory to our understanding of ourselves and of others. The social station is the position that we assume in the division of labor in society. It raises the problem of our mutilation in the form of the relation between our inner and our outer worlds, between our idea of ourselves as godlike and our continuing experience of belittlement.

A course of life results most commonly from the cumulative effects of individual decisions taken against the background of what may be the unforgiving constraints of society. These constraints distribute life chances unequally in every society that has existed up to now. To this day, every society has been a class society, using the family as the instrument for the unequal distribution of economic and educational advantage. In no social order up to now has meritocracy been anything more than a counterweight or a complement to the mechanisms of class advantage. To the extent that meritocracy weakens those mechanisms, it does so only to strengthen the influence of the unequal natural endowments with which each of us is born.

Within these daunting constraints, the individual stumbles half-consciously upon a direction as he forsakes possibilities of action for the sake of a given path. He may continue to conceive other lives and the possibilities of experience accompanying them. Through heroic will or by the play of luck and misfortune, he may even occasionally succeed in changing the course of his life. One day, however, he begins to realize that the life he is living will be the only life he will ever live. He may resign himself to this reality, confirming the reduction of the universal to the particular as well as the insult to the condition of embodied spirit. He may dignify his course of life through its association with a socially recognized form of labor (a craft or honorable calling) and take delight in whatever opportunities for proficiency or virtuosity it provides. Or, unable to find solace in either of these alternatives, he may feel trapped. The sentiment of entrapment is one of the characteristic experiences attending the mutilation imposed on the self by a course of life.

A first antidote to the belittling effect of mutilation is the acceptance of a particular idea of work: work as a transformative vocation. Its hallmark is the relation that it establishes between self-transformation and social reconstruction. We strive to reshape some part of our institutional or conceptual setting, and often fail. Despite our failure, we may succeed in changing ourselves. This stands in contrast to work as an honorable calling and work as instrumental. In the former, the individual's identity comes to be bound up with the performance of this role and he earns a living in a way that also ennobles him. Society teaches the individual to embrace his contingent and particular position and to define his identity by its measure. In the latter, work loses its sanctity and its charm. The individual works only to earn the means with which to sustain value in another realm, typically the family. The combination of the profane work role and the family haven becomes the whole world of the individual. He may hope to sweeten his daily chore but never to transform or transcend it.

A second antidote to the belittling effect of mutilation is engagement in activities that elicit single-mindedness and wholeheartedness. Their objects and occasions may be disproportionate to their devotions. The gap between intensity and its objects was from the beginning the chief sign of our susceptibility to belittlement.

Intensity squandered and misdirected is better than no intensity at all; it affirms and enhances the good of life in the face of death and offers us a temporary release from our groundlessness and insatiability. We can enlist, in the service of an effort to fashion worthier objects, the force that it engenders.

A third antidote to the belittling consequences of mutilation is the development of our ability to imagine the selves that we might have become, not just the selves that might have resulted from paths that we forswore but also those that were always beyond our reach. In choosing a course of life, we renounce many others. In renouncing them, we cease to become the individuals that such courses of life would have shaped. We can nevertheless cultivate the imagination of forms of experience that we renounced, as if developing the power to feel the ghostly movements of missing limbs.

Goethe remarked that there was no crime he might not have committed with slight variations of circumstance. So do we all find ourselves with regard to our fellows, once we come to recognize the effect of our inescapable mutilation upon our shared humanity. Even the answer that the imagination can give to mutilation depends on society. It depends, above all, on the success of education in developing our capacity to imagine the subjective experience of other people in other times and situations. In poetry, in the novel, and in the study of the historical vicissitudes of forms of life and of consciousness, we enhance our capacity to appreciate the diversity of human experience. We come to grasp the truth that humankind develops its powers by developing them in different directions, expressed in distinct institutional regimes.

Mummification

Another decisive incident in human life is our habitual surrender to the routines of our social circumstance as well as to character, the hardened version of our self. Character and circumstance come together and as we grow older they form around each of us a mummy, within which we die many small deaths. To this diminishment of life we may give the name mummification. We cannot ascend, affirming the good of life and increasing our share in some of the attributes that we ascribe to the divine, unless we avert this threat.

Mummification has two different sides: adaptation to society and surrender to character. One side of mummification is our surrender to routinized roles and practices within a particular social circumstance. Each role comes complete with a built-in script instructing the individual how to speak, feel, and act and leading him to resignation in routine and repetition. The way in which the individual engages the circumstance is shaped according to a series of compromises and restraints that clip the wings of fantasy, including his fantasies of escape and empowerment. He resigns himself to the shell of routine and repetition. At that moment, mutilation turns into mummification, and the individual, failing in hope, wastes life.

There is, however, another side to mummification: the self becomes fixed in habits of mind and behavior. At the limit, this hardened self also provides, like a social role, a script that directs the individual how to think, feel, and act. It destroys the spontaneity and surprise that figure among the marks of life. It substitutes for the indefinite self, with its restless longings and nonconformity to circumstance. If it was once only a mask, the mask becomes the face. When Heraclitus said that character is destiny, he described this calamity as an ineradicable part of the human condition. Its place in the experience of life is, however, less an inalterable fate than it is the consequence of a way of living and of a view of our place in the world.

The two sides of the mummy – our adaptation to society and our surrender to character – come to coexist and even to converge.

Their convergence diminishes us. It denies us the power fully to enter into the possession of life in the present and condemns us to a drowsy simulacrum of existence. It prepares us for death only by killing us in steps. As a result, we cease as well to increase our share in the marks of divinity. By giving our divinity away to the mummy, we also abandon to the mummy our humanity.

The beginning of a response to mummification lies in addressing the role of repetition in our experience. On one hand, there is in fact no life – and no collective existence – without repetition; on the other hand, repetition can be used to escape from repetition. Whatever we have learned how to repeat, we can express in a formula. Whatever we have learned how to express formulaically, we can embody in a physical contraption, a machine. The highest use of the machine in the development of our powers is to undertake on our behalf the work that we have learned how to repeat so that we can preserve time – our greatest and, in a sense, our sole resource – for what we have not yet learned how to repeat. By increasing the role of the nonrepetitious in our experience, we become more human by becoming more godlike.

The organization of society can immensely strengthen the hand of the individual in his effort to defeat mummification. It can do so by satisfying three sets of demands, each of them an aspect of the conception of deep freedom.

The first demand is that the everyday world of work cease to be a realm of humiliation and oppression. Every individual must be assured a universal minimum of resources and opportunities, regardless of the position that he occupies in society. Economically dependent wage labor must gradually cease to be the predominant form of free work and must gradually give way to the higher varieties of free labor, self-employment and cooperation. No human being must be condemned to do the repetitious work that machines can execute.

The second demand is that the individual receive from society an education freeing him from the tyranny of present beliefs and institutions. Such an education gives priority to the skills that enable us to decompose and reconstruct knowledge. It uses information, deeply and selectively, as a tool for the acquisition of analytic and synthetic capabilities.

A third demand is change in the quality and content of our institutional arrangements. The most important of such changes is the reorganization of democratic politics. This entails the creation of a high-energy democracy that dissociates the fragmentation of power (the liberal principle) from the slowing down of politics (the conservative principle), that increases the level of organized popular engagement in public life, that quickly overcomes impasse among branches or powers of government, and that favors the creation, in particular parts of a country or parts of a society, of counter-models of the future. The institutional arrangements of democracy enjoy a natural priority over other exercises of institutional change because they help set the terms on which we can change all other arrangements.

A society and a culture that move in this direction enhance our ability to resist mummification. They keep us awake and recall to us at every moment the good that we too readily forget and abandon. However, just as the reconstruction of the social order cannot spare us our moral ordeal, so too our advance toward a higher form of social life cannot exempt us from the imperative of self-transformation. We then come to the central point in our thinking about mummification: how we should act when culture and society do little to rescue us from our fall or actively conspire in robbing us of life before we die.

SIX CHARACTERISTICS OF A LIFE LIVED AGAINST MUMMIFICATION

The way to avoid surrendering life to the mummy is to live life as a search – a search for people and for a task that we can give ourselves to wholeheartedly. Resistance to mummification requires that we grasp the right relation between these answers and orient the conduct of existence accordingly.

It may seem that such an ideal amounts to a luxury reserved for the small part of humanity that is not ground under by material deprivation and social oppression. Yet the centrality of this concern to all men and women will become clearer as the reign of material scarcity weakens and the bonds of subjugation are loosened. Moreover, even under constraint, a human being in any society is more than what he appears to be. His stratagems of resilience and resistance, driven by the love of our greatest good, foretell another future. Part of his work is to turn that orientation to the future into a changed way of living in the present.

A life characterized by the aims invoked by these arguments will have certain marks. I here identify six such marks of living life so as to resist mummification and experience death only once: resisting a hardening of the self, refusing to identify with any particular social or personal role, becoming both an insider and an outsider, balancing the problem of routinization with surprise, taking on large projects, and achieving a heightened vulnerability. These marks are so intimately connected that they are best seen as different aspects of the same way of living. Any one of them taken in isolation invites misinterpretation. Their significance and their reach become clear in the light of their relation to one another. To achieve them is both a goal of our striving and a confirmation of our success.

First mark: resist hardening of the self

The first mark of this way of living is that it manifests a disposition to resist the hardening of the self in the form of character. This disposition can also be described as the effort to form a character that remains open to the possibilities of life and to the promptings of experience. What is such a character – or anti-character – like? It exhibits a mode of being with the characteristics of surfeit, fecundity, and spontaneity. It works to dissolve the contrast between character and life and to reinvent in the grown man or woman the charms and intensity of the child.

Surfeit and spontaneity make possible renewed surprise and fecundity, the perpetual creation of the new – above all, new experience, new connections, new engagements. The significance of the creation of the new is to show and develop our power to exceed all the determinate circumstances of society, thought, and character and, by so doing, to become more human.

Second mark: refuse role identification

The second mark of such a way of living is the refusal to identify the self with any particular role. This refusal is accompanied by another refusal, that of accepting without resistance and qualification the rules and expectations associated with the role. What stands behind the system of roles is the marriage of a social regime with a cultural vision. The regime embeds cooperation in hierarchy. The vision translates the abstract idea of society into a series of models of human association, prescriptive views of how people can and should deal with one another in different domains of social life. The social role contains the regime and the vision within itself. To accept it is to accept them. Such an acceptance represents a denial of the most important fact about our relation to these structures of society and culture: that we exceed, in power and reach, these collective creations of ours and cease to be fully human and alive if we take them as an absolute frame of reference for our striving and thinking.

To a greater or lesser extent, we must tear up the script. We cannot do so without disappointing others who rely on that script. With roles go loyalties. In defying roles, we signify our intention to put under stress the loyalties with which they are associated. We do so up to the limit of personal betrayal, which we must risk crossing when we set out on a defiant and transformative course.

We must perform the roles that exist while enlisting them in the service of ends that they were never designed to support. We must maintain an inner distance from them even as we try in good faith to perform them. We must struggle to reinvent the role the better to enact a vision or to foreshadow another future. By performing them and resisting them at the same time, we become larger and more alive. We cannot do so, however, without causing trouble to others and to ourselves.

Third mark: become both insiders and outsiders

The third mark generalizes the significance of our two-sided relation to social roles: we must be both insiders and outsiders to the regimes of society and thought in which we participate. To be an insider is to think and feel as if the order of life or of thought in which we engage resembled a natural language suitable to the expression of every thought worth thinking. It is to act as the committed functionaries of that world, taking its assumptions about the valuable and the dangerous as well as about the real and the possible as if they were our sole reliable basis for insight and judgment. Conversely, to be an outsider is to chafe under the rule of an ordering of life or thought and to experience such a regime as alien, alien because inadequate to what most needs doing, or making, or inventing, or imagining, or experiencing. It is therefore as well to refuse conformity and to act either to revise or to subvert this order.

In his manner of being both insider and outsider, the individual shows how living for the future can become a way of living in the present as a being for whom circumstance can never have the final say. The tension between being an insider and an outsider helps undermine any equilibrium in the self that has as its requirement the containment or suppression of vitality. It works to enhance life and to dissolve the mummy. Life then becomes prophetic without ceasing to be ordinary. It is the type of prophecy suitable to democracy.

Fourth mark: resist routine

A fourth mark of a life lived so that death happens only once is the way in which such a life addresses the relation between the formulaic and the anti-formulaic elements in our activity. The virtues are habitual predispositions to do the good. But if the virtues were no more than habits, even if directed to right ends, they would signal the surrender of experience to routine. They would serve mummification rather than acting to dissolve the mummy. In the religion of the future, we come to see these habitual predispositions as means by which to affirm in daily life the truth that there is more in each of us than there is in the structures of society and of thought that we inhabit. The virtues of connection take on a preparatory meaning and cease to be the centerpiece of the moral life. As they dethrone us from our self-centeredness, they prepare us for a life of searching in which we are rescued rather than doomed by our dependence on other people. The virtues of purification draw us to the parts of our experience that are least susceptible to being made formulaic; by disengaging us from the peripheral, they equip us to resist the context. The virtues of divinization are habits against habits and against structures.

These last virtues present the most difficult problem in the vision animating the campaign against mummification: the relation of transcendence to solidarity, of greatness to love. We must defy structures to respect people and to make ourselves more fully into the structure-transcending agents that in our actual historical circumstance we only dimly are. However, no defiance of structure is achieved without a threat to solidarity and no greatness is a substitute for love. In all these domains, the task is to change the nature and place of routine and repetition in our experience. The solution is not to devise another theory; it is to live in a different way and to organize society and culture on different terms.

Fifth mark: pursue large projects

The fifth mark of a human existence escaping the mummy is its inclination to conceive and determination to pursue large projects – indeed, the largest project in which the individual, given his situation, his gifts, and his beliefs, can imagine himself passionately engaged. Such a project may be individual or collective. It may be capable of fulfillment in biographical or only in historical time. If it is a collective endeavor that can be achieved only in historical time, the individual may play only a small part in its progress. Nevertheless, that part must be large for him: it must provide him with a task and a struggle that engage him wholly and speak with an authority that no preset social role can possess.

The clearest instance of such a project arises, in modern experience, in the context of a view of work that is characteristic of the freest and most innovative societies in the last few centuries: the idea of the transformative vocation. According to this idea, we are most fully ourselves when we seek to change some part of the world. World transformation, always piecemeal and fragmentary, and always subject to the adventures of unintended consequences, may succeed or fail. In seeking to change the world, we change ourselves. The most important change is that we break the spell of the routinized existence that was willed on us by the alliance between chance and society. We live as if the new were not only feasible but also in our power to make.

Sixth mark: be vulnerable

The sixth mark of a life graced with the power to break out of the mummy is that it shows an acceptance of a heightened vulnerability for the sake of dying only once. The two large families of experiences serving this purpose are love and work, especially love among equals, freely given and freely rebuffed, and work looming large in the consciousness of the self because it elicits its capacity for more intense experience and drives a person to more exertion and greater struggle than any cold calculus of advantage can justify. These two sets of experiences subject us to disappointment, defeat, and derision. We cannot give ourselves to them without at least partly lifting our defenses against other people, despite our ambivalence to them. The cost of entry into these experiences is to tolerate a greater vulnerability to other people.

This price is evident in love, in the love among people who stand, with respect to the experience of love, on an equal plane, no matter how differently the world may view them. The imposition of this tariff represents a sign of the superiority of such love to the disinterested benevolence, given from a distance and from on high, that the most influential traditions of moral thought throughout world history have generally and falsely regarded as the gold standard of human relations. In a more subtle form, the price is charged as well in all the experiences attending the higher forms of cooperation. The most promising cooperative practices are the ones that require us to work together without a rigid allocation of role and responsibility or a stark contrast between supervision and implementation. They impose greater vulnerability because they require higher trust. What counteracts this exposure is the assurance of rights and endowments not dependent upon keeping any particular job.

Such love supplies an antidote to the mummy. It requires that we lower our defenses. A state of greater vulnerability plays an even larger part in our arousal to a larger life than this requirement may suggest. To experience such an ascent, we must be ready for it: we must make ourselves patiently and hopefully available to new engagements and new connections. This patient and hopeful availability draws a broad penumbra of accessible engagement and attachment around our core experiences of work and love. Like those core experiences, it opens us to disappointment. It is nevertheless indispensable because it enables us to change and to escape the hold of the character on the self.

BECOMING MORE HUMAN BY BECOMING MORE GODLIKE

It falls to the religion of the future, in enacting this agenda, to accomplish what the other orientations failed to achieve: teaching us how we can make ourselves both greater and sweeter. In this endeavor it has a formidable ally, democracy, understood as a set of institutions and a system of belief. For democracy allied with the imagination can help accomplish what Christianity and romanticism have left undone. Both as an institutional order and as a public culture, democracy enables us to turn the tables on structure, to give practical effect to faith in the constructive genius of ordinary men and women, and to lay the groundwork for the higher forms of cooperation.

The response to the formative incidents of mutilation and mummification discussed in this chapter tells the story of our ascent through change in the conduct of life chiefly from the perspective of our greatness rather than from the standpoint of our reconciliation. But just as these two sides of the ideal are combined politically in the conception of deep freedom, so too they must be combined morally in a view of the conduct of life. To the extent that they are so combined in both politics and morals, we will be justifiably encouraged. We will recognize the reasonableness of our hope to become more human and godlike, to enter more fully into the possession of life, and to be restored to our selves.

CONCLUSION

Life Itself

IN THE END, all we have is life right now. The roots of a human being lie in the future more than they do in the past, according to the religion of the future. Prophecy counts for more than memory, hope for more than experience, surprise for more than repetition. Time matters more than eternity.

We live for the future, in the light of the future. However, a formative paradox of the religion of the future is that living for the future amounts to a way of living in the present as a being who is more – and who is capable of more – than his situation countenances or reveals. By so reorienting our lives, we are rewarded. Our reward does not rescue us from either mortality or groundlessness. It does not console us for death. It fails even to prepare us for death, as the *Phaedo* wanted philosophy to do. It cannot overcome or diminish the unfathomable and dreamlike character of our existence.

THE REWARD

What then is our reward for reorienting in the direction that I have described as the conduct of life against the background of an effort to secure the conditions for deep freedom? Our reward is to be better able to act single-mindedly and wholeheartedly in the world without giving in to the world. Our reward is a better chance to connect with other people. Our reward is recognizing and accepting others as the context-shaped and context-transcending individuals that all of us are – the class-, race-, gender-, role-transcending individuals that we are – without forfeiting our separateness and our hiddenness. It is also to enlarge the invisible circle of love by which we are all bound, even when we fail to love beyond the closed horizon of our acquaintances.

Our reward is life, death-bound but brought to a higher level of intensity so long as we live. It is the chance to die only once, to possess life right now, wide awake, in the moment – this is the overriding aim of our self-transformation. To this end, we need to reject the ideal of serenity through invulnerability that shaped the moral philosophy of the ancients and through that ideal penetrated the moral beliefs that have prevailed in much of the world over the last few centuries. We must replace it with a view that accepts a heightened vulnerability as the condition of a greater self.

Our reward is the manifest and manifold world to which we would not surrender but rather come to possess more fully as nature and cosmos. Possessing the world more fully means lightening the weight of the categorical schemes through which we see and interpret it. It means affirming our powers of transcendence in our relation to our methods and presuppositions as well as to our institutions and practices. It means hoping that humanity will have a wider part in the experience of genius, which is a power of vision more than it is a capability of reasoning.

Such results will be both causes and consequences of the intensification of experience. It will be the concentration of life, right now. This is the only response to mortality and groundlessness for which, by the light of the religion of the future, we are entitled to hope.

ELEMENTS OF THE RELIGION OF THE FUTURE

The moral and political direction for which I have argued has four elements. These elements of the religion of the future are a confrontation with the flaws of human existence, the conduct of life, the reformation of society, and the promise. I now represent them in a different order from that in which I presented them earlier.

First element: confronting the flaws of human existence

The first element is confrontation with the unavoidable flaws in the human condition. We acknowledge them and face them to the end of living for real in the moment. By this turn, religion becomes something different from what it has usually been in the history of humanity, namely, an effort to console us for our death and groundlessness. This reckoning with the reality of our situation is the turn of pure terror, by which we put away religion as consolation and instead seek religion as a response to existence informed by a more comprehensive view of reality. The terror amounts to an overthrow of the guarded and resigned self by itself. Call this part of the proposal the overthrow.

Second element: conduct of life

A second element in this view of a future religion is the reorientation of the conduct of life. This part of the argument is the heart of the message, presented here in two of its many possible forms:

a conception of the virtues and a response to certain formative incidents in an ordinary human life. Both versions of the message are animated by the same idea of the person as embodied spirit. Both remain faithful to the view of spirit and structure and of self and others for which I have argued: the suppressed and truncated orthodoxies that the religion of the future inherits from the salvation religions as well as from democracy, romanticism, and the other secular projects of political and personal liberation.

This view is a moral conception but not an ethical theory in the conventional sense of academic moral philosophy. It deviates from the path of that philosophy in form as well as in substance. Its aim is not to lay down rules or to show how we can acquit ourselves of our obligations to others the better to appear blameless before the tribunal of conscience. It refuses to take as its guiding concern the taming of our selfishness, although it does assign a central place to the relation between vitality and solidarity. Its attention is focused first and foremost on the enhancement of life, so much so that it may seem not to be a moral view at all. Nevertheless, its implications for our beliefs about how to live soon become apparent. Call this part of the proposal the transformation of the self, or simply the transformation.

Third element: reforming society

A third element of a future religious revolution is its proposal for the reformation of society. It is a direction, not a blueprint. This is what I have argued under the name deep freedom. In opposition to the political ideas that have most recently guided ideological controversy around the world, it combines a devotion to the empowerment of the ordinary person – a raising up of ordinary life to a higher plane of intensity, scope, and capability – with a disposition to reshape the institutional arrangements of society in the service of such empowerment.

This view denies that the cause of economic, political, and social pluralism is adequately served by the institutions that now stand as expressions of the market economy, representative democracy, and independent civil society. It proposes a trajectory of institutional change designed to support what it describes as the higher forms of cooperation. More than any particular way of organizing society, what it wants is to establish a structure that redeems its unavoidable partiality – its tilting toward some forms of experience and against others – through its strengthened corrigibility. It does not try to describe a definitive structure; it proposes movement toward a structure that organizes its own revision. It does not demand surrender as the price of engagement or turn crisis into the condition of change. It provides us with a secular approximation to the ideal of being in the world without being of it.

Fourth element: the promise

The fourth element concerns what a future spiritual revolution promises. At many moments in this argument, I have described this promise in different but equivalent words: the enhancement of life, or possessing it more fully; living for the future in a way that overcomes our estrangement from the present; broadening our share in some of the attributes that we ascribe to God; enacting the truth of embodied spirit as transcendent over the contexts of life and thought that it builds and inhabits; and dying only once. In the previous section, I offered a summary view of this promise as it is expressed in four domains of existence: our response to the institutional and conceptual structures that we ordinarily take for granted, our dealings with one another, the relation of each of us to the settled form of his own self, and our way of the seeing the world around us and of answering the prompts of perception and experience. It was no more than a summary; the vision of this promise runs through the entire argument of this book. Call this fourth part of the proposal the reward.

No simple combination exists among the four elements of the proposal: the overthrow, the transformation, the reconstruction, and the reward. There are disharmonies among them. From the disharmonies, risk and suffering result. These disharmonies and their consequent risks and sufferings have to do with the nature of our existence. The irreparable flaws in the human condition are their ultimate basis. We should recognize them for what they are and refuse the theoretical sleights of hand that would explain them away. In so doing, we renew the marriage of vision and realism on which any religion of the future must draw.

LIFE ITSELF

We live in an age of disillusionment. We may fail to become disillusioned with disillusionment. Political and religious prophets will nevertheless arise. They will undertake what we failed to accomplish. I have suggested what I believe to be the direction – not the doctrine – of the revolution of which we now stand in need. I have described it here chiefly from the standpoint of religion and only secondarily from the perspective of politics, or of politics only insofar as it forms part of religion. The expressions that the religion of the future may have in common with the forms of past religious revolution are only in the combination of visionary teaching and exemplary action. Everything else is bound to be different, so different that it may at first be unrecognizable as the revolution that it is.

The simple, central teaching of the revolutionaries will, nevertheless, be one that we can already hear and heed. We shall soon die and waste away and be forgotten – although we feel that we should not. We shall die without having understood what this indecipherable world and our brief time within it signify.

Our religion should begin by acknowledging these terrifying facts, not by denying them as religion traditionally has done. It should arouse us to change society, culture, and ourselves so that we become – all of us, not just a happy few – bigger as well as more equal and take for ourselves a larger share in powers that we have assigned to God. It should make us more willing to unprotect ourselves for the sake of bigness and of love. It should convince us to exchange serenity for searching.

Then, so long as we live, we shall have a greater life, draw farther away from the idols but closer to one another, and be deathless, temporarily.

APPENDIX

Christianity as the Religion of the Future?

SUPPOSE THAT A PERSON who has found light and guidance in Christianity has taken to heart the criticism of the struggle with the world and understood the reasons that argue for religious revolution now. He understands that the chief aim of this spiritual transformation is to enter more fully into the possession of life, or to achieve a greater life, not just later but right now, so that living for the future becomes a way of living in the present.

He first wants to discover, however, whether this religious change can be accomplished if not within the bounds of his faith, at least with the materials that it provides. Anxious to free himself from error about what matters most, he has opened himself to the religious criticism, no matter how radical, of religion – of his religion. He has faced, without lying to himself or seeking refuge in confusion and sloth, each of the scandals of reason committed by his faith. He has understood how his faith, once interpreted and refined, can be made less scandalous to reason. He nevertheless appreciates that it cannot cease to be scandalous without losing its grip on the vision and the experience that made it powerful in the first place. He has been sobered by reflecting on the influence of circumstance upon belief. This reflection has led him to persist in his spiritual search lest he allow his religious imagination to be ruled by the accidents of family, society, and culture and so license the dead to govern the living. He will not abide such a perversion in this, the most encompassing part of his convictions: the part that connects his vision of our place in the world with his choice of a way to live.

He will then want to understand what in the past and present of Christianity serves and what impedes the needed religious revolution. Whether the religion that results will be seen as the old religion made new or as a new religion altogether is something that, reflecting on the history of Christianity, of its relation to Judaism, of its reformation, and of the faiths that it helped inspire, he knows himself powerless to tell in advance. He hopes that Christianity can itself become the religion of the future. But he hopes even more that the experience of this struggle may help men and women not just in the future but also right now become more human by becoming more godlike.

Thus the question: by what set of changes might Christianity become the religion of the future? First, it would need to respond to the experiences that give cause for religious revolution today, namely, the arousal in humanity of the idea of our own greatness, leading us to pursue the aim of increasing our share in the attributes of the divine, as well as the realization that we cannot become free and ascend to a greater life if we continue to deny the ineradicable defects in human existence. The religion of the future must be able to contain the spiritual ambitions of humanity today and not remain obscured in the limitations of a past where the dead rule over the living. It cannot do so without overcoming the estrangement from the present that has marked it ever since its emergence two thousand years ago. The resultant religion would not be a minor adjustment in belief. It would be a reformation of Christianity more radical than the one that Luther began. The question remains, however, whether we can imagine taking the established religion as the point of departure for such a revolution in our spiritual life.

This appendix examines the question of the possibility of Christianity as the religion of the future. It argues neither for nor against this possibility but raises the specter of necessary reform that would radically remake the Christian religion. In this line of consideration, four key aspects are explored: the halfway house between belief and disbelief; the scandals of reason within Christianity; obstacles inherent to Christian orthodoxy, namely, compromises with existing societies and with Greek philosophy; and, lastly, the potentials of and problems with a dominant heterodox line of thought. In addressing these aspects, it remains an open question whether a reformed Christianity could remain Christianity at all.

THE HALFWAY HOUSE

The halfway house results from lack of both courage and clarity in addressing the difficulty that ever-larger numbers of people experience in bringing themselves to believe in narratives of God's saving intervention in human and natural history. Wanting to believe, they deliver themselves to the sentimental will to believe. They believe as much as they can. They welcome whatever minimalist reinterpretation of their faith may enable them to continue to believe, with the least possible disturbance of their everyday realism.

Such a reinterpretation will pretend to represent a halfway house between belief and disbelief. It will translate the story of God's saving work and of his transactions with humanity into a series of secular ideas about our lives and our dealings with one another. Nothing offensive to reason will remain in the faith, once its narratives have been reinterpreted as an allegory of our secular commitments and aspirations. The believer nevertheless insists that the reduced or sanitized faith is more than a compendium of the secular pieties comprising the text of the reductive translation.

Jesus Christ, for example, was not literally God incarnate. Neither, however, was he just a man like you and me; he was a concentrated embodiment of divine energy. What, however, is divine energy? It is the activity of spirit that we find in our experience of transcendence and that we rediscover at work in evolving nature. It is nonsensical to suppose that we will be resurrected from the dead as the flesh and blood individuals that we are, settling once again into our organisms, once decayed but now reconstituted. However, death cannot be the end. An indescribable sequel awaits us. And so forth.

The pretense of the halfway house is that, after all the justified translation has been accomplished, something of the original story remains, something that we cannot treat as merely allegorical and to which a thoroughly naturalistic discourse fails to do justice. What this extra something is that distinguishes the supposedly decoded religion from its rationalizing counterpart remains unspoken.

There are two major objections to this halfway house between belief and disbelief. Either of them is fatal. Together, they condemn the halfway house as apostasy in the eyes of a believer and as self-deception at the service of temporizing in the estimation of a nonbeliever.

The first objection to the halfway house is cognitive. It is dishonest and self-deluded. There is no real or legitimate halfway house. The halfway house is loss of faith disguised as faith within the bounds of reason. God's revelation is not self-interpreting, because it was given and received in particular historical contexts. That which is due to the context must be separated, as best the believer can distinguish it, from what is instinct to the divine message. Nothing, however, can bridge the gulf between the world as it looks without God's revelation and the world as it becomes and appears in the light of his creative presence and redemptive activity.

The second objection to the halfway house is practical but not on that account any less powerful than the first. Once the work of demythologizing is accomplished, the doctrinal residue will be found to be the conventional moral and political pieties of the age in which it was practiced. It is, consequently, superfluous. No one needs such a translation of the sacred voice into the profane one.

Both the sacred and the profane forms of the struggle with the world retain the potential to resist established arrangements and ideas. They could not otherwise have helped inspire the secular programs of democracy and romanticism that have aroused humanity over the last two centuries. Although the translation of the sacred voice into the profane will seem plausible and persuasive to many, it will be embraced with relief only because it has an outcome that they already approve and await. It will attract no interest and exert no force if it claims that the redeemer simply prefigured the teaching of some contemporary moral or political reformer or anticipated the dogmas of our culture and the illusions of our age. A shared collective view must be there on the other side: the standards of good behavior embraced by the prudent and the worthy; the theoretical universalism, altruism, and egalitarianism of the political and moral philosophers; devotion to family and country; respect for the job – everything that the religion of the crucified God, received without the hemming and hawing of the halfway house between belief and disbelief, might better be thought to threaten and contradict.

THE SCANDALS OF REASON

Once we have set aside the confusions of the halfway house between belief and disbelief, we can face the chief objection to taking seriously the sacred voice of the struggle with the world: the scandals of reason. The scandals of reason shadowing the salvation religions are three: the scandal of supernaturalism, the scandal of particularity (a universal message attributed to a particular plot: the narrative of divine intervention and revelation in particular times and places), and the scandal of the incoherence or unintelligibility of the idea of God – at least of any version of that idea that can do the work required of it by one of the salvation religions. Consider these scandals of reason from the perspective of the argument against the halfway house between belief and disbelief and in Christian context. The point is to determine on what terms or in what sense someone who confronts these scandals can give them their due, without the equivocations of the halfway house, and nevertheless begin the required religious revolution within the confines of the established religion.

The scandal of supernaturalism is the role that is played in the narratives of Christianity – as in those of the other salvation religions – by initiatives and events that defy the regular workings of nature, those causal connections and the laws that ordinary perception observes or that science discovers. Having created the world, God periodically intervenes in it. His interventions may suspend all regular causal connections as well as work through them. The power to interrupt or to change the normal workings of nature may occasionally be invested in particular individuals – saints – as a sign of their greater sharing in the life of God. The Incarnation, the virgin birth of Christ, and the resurrection of the body (beginning with the resurrection of the body of Christ) are all instances within Christianity of such supernaturalism. They are opposed to the rationalist or deist conception of a God who remains silently and passively apart from the workings of his created nature.

No dialectic between observation and theorizing could ever reconcile us to such a supernaturalism. Only a tremendous event, possessing the power to recognize personalities and events that establish new orders of meaning and of experience, could produce such an effect. It is vision inspired by an encounter that lies at the heart of such epiphanies: coming face to face with a reality or a teaching that is felt to be irresistible.

The second scandal of reason is the scandal of particularity. It arises from the strangeness of the conveyance of a universal message by particular individuals at particular times and in particular places. Why did God assign a major role to the Jews in his plan of salvation? Why did he become incarnate as a Palestinian Zealot in a minor province of the Roman Empire during the reign of Augustus? Why was the meeting of Judaism with Hellenism in the early history of this religion allowed to exert an influence out of all proportion to the confrontations among other cultures in other ages? Why did the human embodiment of God not take place earlier, to the spiritual benefit of the many dead who were denied the light, or later, at a time when the message might have been less likely to be perverted by compromise with Roman imperial power?

The plot is particular. The message is universal. We can go a long distance in providing a wholly secular account and defense of this attribution of a universal meaning to a singular plot. The narrative of salvation is organized around the points of inflection and rupture at which God breaks into human history and brings new tidings and new chances for experience to the human race. The personalities active at these turning points – the incarnate God and those whose lives he begins to touch in ever-wider concentric circles – are the authors of a new way of living and seeing. The events have a meaning that outreaches their immediate context.

There is a vast and immeasurable distance between these claims and the idea of exemplary individuals and events in history. Nothing can bridge this gap. The existence of natural and historical counterparts to the scandal of particularity fails to diminish its power to perplex and to disturb.

The third scandal of reason is the scandal of divine existence. It concerns the inadequacy and incoherence of the ideas of God that are available to the Christian, as to the Jew or the Muslim. The idea of God as person is suggested by the narrative of salvation. In Christianity, it is made indispensable by the Incarnation. What no believer can grasp, however, is how God can be both a person and a being radically transcendent over the world and therefore incomparable to any part of our finite existence. Moreover, the view of God as person can never be wiped clean of the taint of an anthropomorphic projection. In this sense, it seeks to contain the infinite within the finite. It verges on idolatry.

The idea of God as being is free from this taint. It achieves this freedom, however, only at the cost of conflicting with the narrative of God's creative and saving work and of affirming the primacy of the impersonal over the personal. Impersonal being cannot be the living God. It is the God of the philosophers, not the God of Abraham or of the New Testament. The embrace of the idea of God as impersonal being leads to one or another form of panentheism, if not monistic pantheism. For the monist or the pantheist, God and world are one and the same. For the panentheist, God constitutes the world, or the world God, but God as impersonal being is the world plus something else. This something else may be imagined spatially and spiritually as a reality that exceeds manifest nature. Panentheism is, however, powerless to bring us to the promise of salvation that is central to the Christian faith. It cannot connect to the particular events that comprise, in this faith, the narrative of redemption, from the covenant with Israel to the advent, passion, and resurrection of the redeemer and the continuation of his work by the Church. This whole story fades away at the instigation of an impersonal idea of God into a spiritual allegory that the residue of historical fact underlying it is unable to support.

There remains a third idea of God that bids for supremacy: God as nonperson and nonbeing, a God who is the ground of being because he is radical negation. Such is the idea of God that has always been attractive to mystics within Christianity as well as Judaism and Islam. It is less a conception of God than it is a confession of our inability, as believers, to achieve any such conception. It borders on heresy: first, because it implies that the story of creation and salvation, expressed as it is in the language of personal experience and encounter, must be given a meaning far from its literal significance and, second, because the powerlessness of reason to parallel at least part of the faith in revelation leaves the message of salvation as an empty vessel that we can fill with whatever we will, as if the presentiment of our impending annihilation in a world that we are unable to comprehend could be displaced by the anticipation of a last-minute, unaccountable rescue.

The inadequacy or incoherence of each of these available ideas of God poses a fundamental threat to the faith. It places the believer's will to believe at odds with his understanding. It inverts the ontological argument for the existence of God, undermining grounds for belief in a (non)being who is not even thinkable. In natural science, we may find reason to believe in variations of reality that overstep the limits of our perceptual experience. However, we take our intellectual and spiritual lives in our hands when we fabricate an abstraction of which our own reasoning is unable to make sense.

CHRISTIAN ORTHODOXY AND OBSTACLES TO THE REVOLUTIONARY CAUSE

The main line of Christian orthodoxy presents two connected obstacles to the revolutionary cause. The first is the compromise of the Christian faith – and of the Church as its agent – with the regimes prevailing in the societies in which Christianity has been believed and practiced. The second is the marriage of Christian philosophy, centered on God's dramatic intervention in history, with Greek philosophy, organized around the category of being.

Compromise with society

As a religion of immanence and transcendence, Christianity must not leave society alone. It must have a proposal for the remaking of our earthly state and insist that the work of salvation begins in historical time. The commitment to particular requirements and prohibitions, such as those regarding the sanctity of life from the time of conception or the indissolubility of the sacramental bond of marriage, are far from presenting a comprehensive view of the form that our life in society should take. The social doctrine of the Church, as exemplified by the encyclicals of the Roman pontiffs or by the social gospel of the Reformed churches, offers no reliable model of social organization. It has regularly veered between a defense of social and economic rights, bereft of the institutional machinery that would ensure their effective exercise, and an institutional blueprint, like the communitarian corporatism of the papal encyclicals of the interwar period in the twentieth century, that was soon discredited and abandoned.

As an organized religion and community of faith, Christianity has struck two thousand years of compromises with a series of social regimes and forms of consciousness. These, rather than the largely empty or misguided abstractions of the moral philosophers, have been the chief shapers of moral experience in all the societies and cultures in which Christianity has exercised a paramount influence. The feudal ethic of chivalry and the Victorian ethic of pious self-restraint and responsibility represent two examples among many of such a transaction between Christian faith and social order. In each instance, the faith enters into the order, softening its cruelties and raising its sights. In each, however, the order also enters into the faith, dulling its subversive and transformative power and committing it to arrangements that conflict with the tenets of the religion.

Always and everywhere, the settlement has included the acceptance of the structures of class society. It has respected the established assignment of social roles as a basis for our obligations to one another. It has accepted the present form of the division of labor and the prevailing social order as the template for the discharge our obligations to one another.

Nothing in such compromises, or in their consequences, can be reconciled with the core of the faith. The undoing of these deals would amount to a momentous change in the character and presence of the faith. Such a Christianity does not exist, and it has never existed, despite the many occasions in the history of Christian societies in which the faith has sparked collective movements of enthusiasm and insurrection and despite the counter-models of social life and personal piety in which (thanks to monasticism and evangelism) the history of Christianity has been prodigal.

The fundamental issue at stake in this conflict between religious faith and social compromise is the extent of our hope of living in the world as who we really are and who we discover ourselves to be rather than as placeholders in a system of social classes and roles. If triumph over the experience of susceptibility to belittlement is, together with the overcoming of estrangement from life in the present, a major incitement to new religious revolution, then Christianity can vie to be the religion sought by that revolution only if it puts an end to this history of compromise and replaces it by another idea of politics.

Compromise with Greek philosophy

Just as Christianity has been compromised by society, it has also been compromised by philosophy. From very early in the transition from the teachings of Jesus of Nazareth, Christianity was wedded to Greek philosophy and to the philosophical tradition that descends from the ancient Greeks. The marriage of Christian faith to Greek philosophy is not an accidental or peripheral feature of Christianity. Once Christianity had ceased to be the original teaching of Jesus of Nazareth, it took up with the Johannine and Hellenistic philosophy of the logos. Philosophy informed the orthodox view of the central mysteries of the Incarnation and the Trinity as established by the early councils that set the path of orthodoxy, and it guided the teachings of the most influential exponents of theological orthodoxy. Today we continue to have no clear purchase on what the Christian faith would be like if it were purged of its translation into the categories of Greek philosophy.

The problem that this reckoning with Greek philosophy presents for Christianity is not confined to Platonism and to the Platonic demotion of the reality of time and of the significance of history. The problem lies, rather, in the more fundamental assertion of the superior reality and value of impersonal being over personality and personal encounter. What runs through the philosophical tradition that set its mark on Christianity, as it did on modern science, is the project of classical ontology: the effort to ground our understanding of the world in a basic and lasting structure. However, it is part of the metaphysical impulse of Christianity, as an expression of the struggle with the world, to affirm the inclusive reality of time, the ascendancy of the personal over impersonal being, and the idea that no structural division of the world lasts forever. Moreover, it is not impersonal being but rather our dealings with one another – as well those we have with God, conceived on the model of personal encounter – that represent, in this religion, the decisive events in the trajectory of humankind.[22]

This influence of Greek philosophy works to undermine the integrity and suppress the efficacy of the twin ideas that represent the most important legacy of Christianity to the religion of the future: the ideas of self and others and of spirit and structure explored earlier in this book.

THE AXIS OF HERESY

I turn now from the main line of Christian orthodoxy to the long-lasting source of tension and movement within Christianity, which we might call the axis of heresy, except that it has been one of the sources of the religion in every period of its history back to its very origin.

The tendency to which I refer is the one that begins in Paul, continues through Augustine, receives a consummation of sorts in Luther and Calvin, and is explored comprehensively in the theologies of Schleiermacher and Barth as well as in the religious practice of latter-day evangelical Protestantism. It has accompanied the entire history of Christianity as the shadow of orthodoxy. It would be strange to call it an axis of heresy, because its founder, Paul, is regarded by many as the real author of the religion, the religion about the Son of Man, as distinguished from the teaching of Jesus of Nazareth. Yet if it is not heresy, it is the perennial source of schism, given that little time ever passes before the conventional Christianity of the organized churches is found wanting by its standards. It therefore appears at the gate with the double face of orthodoxy and heresy.

Two large themes persist throughout the evolution of the religious thinking of these schismatics. The first is the priority of faith over reason: we cannot reason ourselves to salvation; we must be taken by storm and find ourselves, under the burdens of mortality, groundlessness, and insatiability, confronted with an assault of the divine on our natural experience. The second theme is our radical dependence on the living and active God: our inability to lift ourselves up and to cure ourselves by our own devices of the wounds of death, darkness, and longing for the absolute.

As the first theme is described by the formula of faith over reason, the second theme is represented as grace over works – its psychological hallmark, however, is pure terror, followed by the discovery of a source of inexplicable and unjustified salvation. The terror results from awareness of our haplessness, not simply with regard to the forces of nature, as was true of the religions that preceded the past wave of religious revolution, but with respect to the irreparable defects in the human condition, to which all the religions resulting from those revolutions respond. From this radical vulnerability we can be rescued, if we are rescued at all, by a power external to nature and to all being. We call this power God.

The inscrutable character of his being, attested by the incoherence or inadequacy of all the available conceptions of his nature, imparts, however, to this rescue a character that remains for the believer as frightening as it may be joyful. It is gratuitous: it bears no correspondence to our merits. It is unfathomable: we have no hope of penetrating the sources of its bestowal. Who will be saved? What will it be like? What relation will our afterlife bear to the earthly life to which we are normally so attached and the approaching annihilation of which appears to us as absolute evil? Thus, the terror accompanying the experience of haplessness carries over to the expectation of the rescue, the waiting period in which we spend our lives.

THE ALTERNATIVE PATH

Consider what resources and impediments this running insurgency within the religion and this major influence on its development offer for the religious change discussed earlier in this book. The first element of this countertradition would need to be radically reinterpreted. The second element would need to be replaced by the extension of an idea drawn from the core of orthodox doctrine.

The part of abiding truth in the priority of faith over reason is the circumstantial character of religious conviction. Only a connection, arising out of love, could make up for the difference. Originally, at the beginning of the religion, this connection may be to the inspired founder or teacher and to the small circle gathered around him. Later it becomes to the community of the faithful, exemplified in the family, in the nation, or in part of the people. The voluntary convert, uninfluenced by the pressures of a mass option, will have heard the message manifest in the visionary teaching and exemplary action of particular individuals. The message must be embodied and become, for those who convey it as well as for those who receive it, a manner of love.

Suppose that we ask the believer, who has been brought up in faith from childhood, or has been led to an alien faith by dint of chance meetings, why he believes. If he is both candid and ardent, if his faith is no mere abasement before the idols of a tribe, he will answer as follows: "I believe because I loved and because I was shaken. I loved my family, my community, or my teacher and received from them or from him the implicit knowledge about great things as well as small ones that cannot be inferred from abstractions. It is not just that I belonged but rather that through belonging I came to believe. My belief found confirmation in my experience of having come to a more vibrant state of being, not just in a promised future but right now. If I am honest about the sources and character of my experience, I must acknowledge that I would likely have held different beliefs had I been born to different parents in a different time and place. The exclusiveness of the truth that I came to embrace matters less to me than its proximity and its power. If you ask me how it compares to the truth entertained by rival religions, I do not know. All I can do is to study them from the outside, to read about them in books, and to find out about them by hearsay, at a second remove. I cannot have of them the inner knowledge that I have of my own faith, unless another set of circumstantial influences and compelling encounters were to carry me in the direction of those other faiths."

What is sacrificed in this view of faith is its claim to exclusivity. It is sacrificed because the intensity of belief and the transformative efficacy of the faith thus embraced do nothing to validate belief in the exclusive truth of the faith. On the contrary, they cast doubt on the claim to exclusivity – a similar experience of compelling connection and transformative belief can happen and has happened, by the countless millions in the spiritual history of humankind, to believers in clashing faiths. The problem is that a decisive weakening or outright relinquishing of the claim to exclusivity is not simply an adjustment to the religion – it is a radical change. It is only one of the radical changes that Christianity would have to undergo if it were to bid for the role of religion of the future.

The second element in the long-standing rebellion within Christianity – the idea of our unlimited dependence on God – would need more than reinterpretation and revision. It would need to be replaced. Surprisingly, the required replacement comes from the center of orthodoxy.

The idea of our limitless dependence on God is incompatible with the vision of any faith that wants men and women to become more human by becoming more godlike. The view that this radical dependence on an inscrutable if loving God is the most decisive feature of the human condition diminishes the significance of our power to transcend and reshape context and to increase our share in some of the attributes of divinity. It cannot serve a religious revolution that takes as one of its points of departure the enhancement of life. It leaves us defenseless against the experience of estrangement from the present.

At the heart of Christian orthodoxy we can find the beginnings of beliefs that we would need to put in the place of the sense of radical dependence. We can find them in the main line of the Christian theologians who, from Athanasius (the chief author of the Nicene Creed) to Thomas Aquinas (the most influential arbiter of Christian theological correctness for centuries), have marked out the path of Christian orthodoxy. This idea is most often developed in the setting of the theology of the Incarnation. Whenever we find it expressed, we may be taken aback, for it seems on its face to be blasphemous. For example, in his sermon on the Feast of Corpus Christi, Aquinas wrote: "Since it was the will of God's only-begotten Son that men should share in his divinity, he assumed our nature in order that by becoming man he might make men gods."

Had not Maximus the Confessor, writing six hundred years before this sermon was delivered, invoked neo-Platonism in the service of a theology of deification, which he regarded as orthodox and which later came to exercise a major influence in the Orthodox Christianity of the East? According to this view, there is an exchange of natures between God and man: if God becomes man by condescension, man becomes, and is called, God by grace.

What distinguishes the sacred from the profane voice in the development of this conception, expressed by Aquinas and foreshadowed by Maximus among many, is the teaching (based on revelation and experience) that our becoming gods is necessarily preceded, and made possible, by God becoming man. Becoming gods, if it is not to mean becoming like the gods of the Greeks and the Romans, untroubled by the want of the infinite, must mean sharing in the life of God. It must mean that we become present to ourselves only by becoming, and by being, more than ourselves. It must mean, to use the language of Nicholas of Cusa, that by becoming God, which is to say, by partaking in his nature, we become identical to ourselves. If we remained only ourselves, we would continue to be separated from ourselves.

If the Christian ceases to believe in the divinity of Christ and ceases to credit the promise of eternal life, inseparable from the self if not from the body, if he views Christ as simply a visionary teacher and exemplary agent inspired by the closeness of his access to the divine, and if he dismisses the expectancy of resurrection as no more than a metaphor for our survival in the collective work of humanity, he has taken refuge in the halfway house between belief and disbelief. He has reduced his faith to an embroidering of beliefs that gain nothing from the allegorical surplus that he appends to it. His religion then becomes an evasion and declines into irrelevance.

If, however, he holds the line at this point, he continues to convey in a sacred voice a message irreducible to the profane version of the religion of the future. He claims to see (to use Karl Rahner's distinction) beyond the lesser hope of a change of life to the greater hope of life forever. He has renounced the claim of exclusive access to salvation without accepting the limits of a secular humanism. He has replaced the idea of our radical dependence on God with a view of our divinization, according to which we can become at once more human and more godlike without mistaking ourselves for God. This religion would be a religion distinct from the Godless version of the religion of the future that I explored in this book. But would it be Christianity?

CHRISTIANITY REFORMED?

No theoretical analysis can determine whether the religion resulting from these revisions would remain Christianity. It would, at the very least, amount to a radical reformation of Christianity, different in character, intention, and effect from the Protestant Reformation. Protestantism represented, among other things, a moment in the deepening of the Pauline and Augustinian tradition or countertradition within Christianity, with its affirmation of our radical dependence on revelation and grace. It maintained the intransigent claim of the faith to offer the exclusive path to salvation and affirmed that Christ is the definitive and sole incarnation of the living God. It persisted in the view, characteristic of all historical Christianity, that the overriding good lies beyond both biographical and historical time. Our earthly experience remains irretrievably broken, despite the presence in our minds and hearts of sanctifying grace. What we undergo and accomplish on earth can at best be a preparation and a prefiguring of a greater change, accomplished only after our lives on earth are over. In all these respects, the religion defined by the changes discussed in the preceding pages would take another course.

Indeed, the changed Christianity that I have explored in these pages may seem to be no Christianity at all. On its face, by the reading of propositions in context, it amounts to a different religion. Whether, however, it is the same or a different religion depends on a contest that has not yet even begun.

Notes

1. Roberto Mangabeira Unger, *The Religion of the Future* (Cambridge: Harvard University Press, 2014), 456.
2. See conclusion of chapter 4.
3. See Cornel West, "Between Dewey and Gramsci: Unger's Emancipatory Experimentalism," in *Critique and Construction: A Symposium on Roberto Unger's Politics*, ed. Robin W Lovin and Michael J Perry (Cambridge: Cambridge University Press, 1990), 256-266.
4. Carlin Romano, "Harvard Law's Roberto Unger Takes on the Future of Brazil," *Chronicle of Higher Education*, June 6, 2008.
5. Unless stated otherwise, all quotes and references are from interviews and conversations with the editor in 2011 and 2012.
6. Eyal Press, "The Passion of Roberto Unger: A Harvard Law Professor Jettisons His Past and Sets Out to Destabilize Latin America," *Lingua Franca*, March 1999.
7. "Guggenheim Gives Fellowships for '76, Unger Gets Tenure, Too," *The Harvard Crimson* April 5, 1976.
8. Some of these different approaches now are liberal jurisprudence (Dworkin), law and economics (Posner), legal process (Hart), and even CLS.

9. The lines of inquiry at the time centered around questions like the role of judges and how they should decide cases, or the power of the supreme court.
10. For more on the CLS movement, see Mark G. Kelman, *A Guide to Critical Legal Studies* (Cambridge: Harvard University Press, 1987). Also see Roberto Mangabeira Unger, *The Critical Legal Studies Movement: Another Time, A Greater Task* (New York: Verso Books, 2015), 3-42. The role of Unger and his ideas in the CLS movement is discussed in Hugh Collins, "Roberto Unger and the Critical Legal Studies Movement," *Journal of Law and Society* 14 (1987), 387–410.
11. Roberto Mangabeira Unger, *The Critical Legal Studies Movement* (Cambridge: Harvard University Press, 1986), 121–122.
12. This similarly transpired in China. Warring States thinkers, from Confucius to Laozi, and their successors, from Xunzi to Dong Zhongshu, grappled with the fundamental questions of existence and social organization, which they effected through direct political action. The obvious examples include the Mohists proselytizing in the marketplace and Hanfeizi advising the Qin state. See E. Bruce Brooks and A. Taeko Brooks, *The Emergence of China: From Confucius to the Empire* (Amherst: Warring States Project, 2015); A. C Graham, *Disputers of the Tao: Philosophical Argument in Ancient China* (La Salle, Ill: Open Court, 1989); Yuri Pines, "Disputers of the 'Li': Breakthroughs in the Concept of Ritual in Preimperial China," *Asia Major* 13, no. 1 (January 1, 2000): 1–41. Beginning in the twelfth century, the Neo-Confucians, facing economic and social upheaval, married a philosophy of self and society with one of political intervention, eventually seizing the reins of power and shaping the course of late imperial Chinese statecraft. See Peter Bol, *Neo-Confucianism in History* (Cambridge: Harvard University Asia Center, 2008).
13. For a discussion of the role of political decay in the formation of political thought, see Hans Morgenthau, "Thought and Action in Politics," *Social Research* 51, no. 1/2 (1984): 143-165.
14. Roberto Mangabeira Unger, "O Brasil depois de Geisel: O pais as tontas" [Brazil after Geisel: The country in a daze], *Folha de Sao Paulo*, January 14, 1979.

15. See William H Simon, "Social Theory and Political Practice: Unger's Brazilian Journalism," *Northwestern University Law Review* 81 (1986-87): 296–332.
16. *ibid.*
17. Roberto Mangabeira Unger, *Social Theory: Its Situation and Its Task* (New York: Verso, 2004 [1987]), 79.
18. Unger often employs these phrases in explanation of his vision of humanity. For example, see his Tanner lectures on religion: https://www.robertounger.com/philosophy-and-religion
19. Unger argues that we have to relate not only to other people but also to the social structures of our world. We must, for example, have institutions that define our material transactions, but, because they are finite and have no definitive form, whereas we are infinite and without a certain resting place, we must always and constantly stand in opposition to these structures. "We can only be true to ourselves and each other by resisting structure," he says.
20. For a development of many of the theses of this metaphysical vision informing the struggle with the world see Roberto Mangabeira Unger and Lee Smolin, *The Singular Universe and the Reality of Time* (Cambridge: Cambridge University Press, 2016). In that work, the conception stands on its own as a position within cosmology and natural philosophy. Its pertinence to the argument of the present book is to suggest how we can not only radicalize this metaphysical vision but also, by radicalizing it, reconcile it with what science has discovered about the workings of nature.
21. This critique of classical social theory and the alternative are expressed in full in Unger's "Politics" series: Roberto Mangabeira Unger, *Social Theory: Its Situation and Its Task* (New York: Verso, 2004); Roberto Mangabeira Unger, *False Necessity: Anti-Necessitarian Social Theory in the Service of Radical Democracy*, Politics, a Work in Constructive Social Theory (New York: Verso, 2004); Roberto Mangabeira Unger, *Plasticity into Power: Comparative-Historical Studies of the Institutional Conditions of Economic and Military Success* (New York: Verso, 2004).

22. To find alternatives to the project of classical ontology, we need to go to some of the pre-Socratics or to a few of the philosophers of the modern West. We need to evoke the Anaximander who wrote: "All things originate from one another and vanish into one another, according to necessity ... under the dominion of time." Or we need to appeal to Pascal, to Kierkegaard, to Bergson, or to twentieth-century philosophers of action and personality, within or outside of Christianity, like Blondel and Levinas. These have not been the philosophical tutors of Christian orthodoxy.

INDEX

D

U

V

W